TO LIVE AND WRITE IN LA

A STREET-LEVEL GUIDE TO SURVIVING AS A SCREENWRITER

JIM AGNEW

DISCLAIMER

Everything in this book is based on my personal experiences, opinions, and how I remember them, which may or may not align with how other people remember the same events.

FOR MORE INFORMATION

CONTENTS

INTRODUCTION

If I'd been born in Kansas City, I'd probably be working the night shift at a meatpacking plant, smelling like blood and regret. But as luck would have it, my parents—barely in their early 20s—packed up everything they owned, climbed into a car and drove from Kansas City to Los Angeles with no real plan.

Growing up in LA County meant Hollywood was always an hour away—close enough to touch, far enough to feel forbidden. As teenagers, we'd pile into some dented Dodge, blast down the freeway and spill out onto Hollywood Boulevard. I watched a movie being shot on Sunset from a street corner. I spotted actors wandering around Santa Monica like it was no big deal. I snuck into dim, smoky dive bars where everyone from Johnny Depp to David Lynch held court.

I stayed cool—never asked for an autograph, never bugged anyone.

I loved films growing up, and I wanted in.

I didn't know if I wanted to be a producer, director or writer, but I knew I wanted to make films—not just watch them. I had no idea where to start. I had zero connections, and when I told my friends I was going to work in movies, they laughed.

Nothing drives me more than being told *no*.

I forced my way into the film business. I was going to make movies one way or another. My first gig was a shitty job at a studio shuffling files. Then I landed a job at a production company—not one that actually produced films, but one that imported anime from Japan. I wasn't at the center of Hollywood yet, but every step kept me industry adjacent.

Eventually, I was hired to help produce a small indie film—a job I was definitely underqualified for, but I bullshitted my way in. I knew just enough to sound like a producer while having absolutely no idea what the job truly required.

That tiny film led to several other producing gigs. They were small, the pay was low but I was learning. One day I'd be a producer on set; the next, I'd be working a temp job to pay rent. I didn't care, as long as I was headed in the right direction.

I was reading a lot of scripts—most of them terrible. One day my confidence flared: *I can write something better than this.*

I was right.

I could write screenplays—and get paid for it. What helped me most in the shift from production to writing was that I already understood the basics of how the industry worked.

That became my advantage, the reason I've been lucky enough to get paid to write screenplays for over 20 years.

I learned everything I could about the film and TV *business.*

CHAPTER 1
THE ITALIAN JOB
(GONE WRONG)

SUNDAY NIGHT, 4:42 am, Torino, Italy. Outside, rain battered the window of my hotel room. I hadn't slept all night. I was dressed in black jeans, black T-shirt and a black leather jacket. My running shoes were tied tight.

I cracked the front door to my room. Down the long, endless hallway, I spied the front counter of the boutique hotel. Perched at the desk was the lone night manager.

He was an absolute machine of a human being—hadn't moved from his post for four hours straight. Just sitting there, mainlining cappuccinos and absorbing mind-numbing Italian television like it was high art. The guy was either deeply committed to his job or afraid to be alone with his thoughts.

Either way, he was fucking up my escape plan.

I checked the time. Now it was 4:46. *Shit. I'm fucked. I need to get out of here.* I cracked the door open again...and then it happened. The night manager was gone. I didn't know where he went. The bathroom? Smoke break?

Either way, this was my chance. I grabbed my bag and made a run for it. I sped through the hallway, past the abandoned front desk. I bolted out the front door. A blast of cold air hit me as I ran down a narrow, rain-drenched Italian back alley. Once I reached the main thoroughfare, I flagged down a taxi.

The obese driver looked stunned that someone wanted a ride so early. "Take me to the airport," is all I said.

As we drove off, I looked through the back window, expecting the night manager to be chasing the cab down the street. But there was nothing besides a drizzle of rain and the hotel's vacancy sign in my rearview.

The reason for my hasty exit?

The producers of the film I'd spent the last three months working on had flaked out on their responsibility of paying my rather large hotel bill. Not a surprise, since they had been cutting corners since day one of filming.

At the airport, I hustled through security, my head on a swivel. I quickly showed my passport and went straight to my gate. My destination was Frankfurt. The German city wasn't a choice so much as an escape hatch—the first flight out that morning to anywhere that wasn't Italy. The plane boarded, and as it sat on the tarmac, I kept waiting for the Italian police to intercept it on the runway. I felt like Billy Hayes from *Midnight Express* as I nervously awaited takeoff. Ninety minutes later, I was in Frankfurt.

A few months earlier, my cinematic dream of getting a screenplay turned into my first film had come true. After years of aborted take-offs and starts and stops...it finally happened. There I was, in Torino, Italy, shooting a film called *Giallo* (*Yellow* in Italian) that was being directed by iconic horror master Dario Argento and starring the Academy Award-winning Adrien Brody.

It was the culmination of over a decade of dreaming and grinding. A screenplay idea born just 18 months earlier was now being brought to life right before my eyes.

Being on set for the entire shoot was a condition of my

contract, a perk I insisted on since the pay was laughably low. The director had requested my presence for any on-the-fly script changes, and I wasn't about to pass up an all-expenses-paid trip to Italy. We wrapped the film after three intense, chaotic months. I was riding high on the euphoria of finally seeing my work translated into celluloid magic.

A day after shooting wrapped, the call came in. One of the producers—a gluttonous figure straight out of central casting, a Frenchman who could out-eat, out-smoke and out-sweat anyone—delivered the gut punch. "We can't pay your hotel bill; you have to cover it," he announced.

The hotel presented me with a €5,000 bill for my stay, which was supposed to be covered by the production. "We told the hotel you'll be paying it, and you can't leave until you do," the Frenchman added before hanging up.

My blood boiled.

I was the reason this film existed, and yet here I was, being stiffed with a massive hotel bill. I asked the other crew members if they were in the same boat. No. Their rooms were covered by the Italian production company. I was the only one left to fend for myself. I later learned that the film had been underfunded and rushed into production, which was why there was a shortage of money to pay bills at the end of the shoot.

After splitting the fee for the script with my writing partner, I'd only made a measly $25,000 (before taxes) for a year and a half's worth of work. I couldn't pay a €5,000 hotel bill. Desperation breeds creativity. So I concocted my escape plan.

A few days later, I had returned to LA. The producer called, irate and spewing invectives. I realized his fury wasn't about the unpaid bill—it was about losing the chance to screw me over.

This is a guy who drove up and down Sunset Boulevard, wedged into a restored 1965 convertible Corvette, chain-smoking $100 cigars. He could have paid my hotel bill, but he didn't want to see that money coming out of his own bottom line.

And that's the first thing you need to know if you want to be a working screenwriter: It's a business. The second thing is that everyone tries to fuck over the writer. If you're a writer, they think you're a creative idiot who doesn't understand the intricacies of how a film is made.

The more you understand about the business side of filmmaking—how films are put together and financed—the easier it will be to navigate this world and not get screwed financially or creatively.

A decade later, that same French producer—after years of all-you-can-eat Brazilian steakhouses and high-end cigars—had a quadruple bypass. I sent him an email wishing him well, despite our past.

Five minutes later, he replied, "Thanks. Send me some scripts. Let's put another film together."

CHAPTER 2
ONCE UPON A TIME
IN LANCASTER

THE DRIVE-IN THEATER rewired my consciousness, though not in any way the family values crowd would approve of. It wasn't through the wholesome Disney fare playing on our designated screen, but the forbidden images bleeding across from the neighboring screens like contraband cinema.

Our desert town's triple-screen drive-in stood like illuminated monoliths against the endless dark, serving as my portal to worlds I had no business seeing.

When my dad and sisters settled in to watch *The Apple Dumpling Gang,* I'd position myself strategically in the back seat, eyes magnetized to the adjacent screen. The sound from the other theater was lost to the night air, but those visuals burned themselves into my young mind with the permanence of a cattle brand.

Before I'd even reached double digits, I had secretly consumed a banquet of exploitation films and midnight movies —material inappropriate for a grade-schooler. I saw them all: *Mad Max*'s dystopian fury, *The Incredible Melting Man*'s grotesque transformation, *The Driller Killer*'s urban stalking nightmare. *Star Wars* may have sparked my love of cinema, but it was the illicit thrill of watching *Rolling Thunder* through a beat-up Mercury Comet's side window that truly sealed my fate.

I learned to stifle gasps and remain perfectly still through sequences like the acid spill in Lucio Fulci's *The Beyond*. I held myself rigid with terror—not from the films, but the possibility that my dad might catch me watching the wrong screen. The drive-in didn't just entertain me; it initiated me into a shadowy world of adult fears, ultraviolence and forbidden knowledge, all while my family munched popcorn in blissful ignorance.

In Lancaster, California—60 miles north of Los Angeles— there wasn't much of anything resembling culture. Entertainment options were exceptionally limited. The drive-in was a beacon of excitement in an otherwise soul-crushing landscape. Tuesday nights transformed into weekly celebrations when the marquee announced "Dollar Night": $1 per carload, a pricing structure that suggested the management either had hearts of gold or terrible business sense.

For families like ours, operating on a very tight budget, this represented an unexpected luxury: taking the kids to movies on a school night. We'd pile into station wagons and pickup trucks, smuggling in Shasta Colas and homemade popcorn like we were running contraband across the border. The drive-in didn't care what you brought—no pretense, no judgment, just honest white-trash entertainment under the vast desert sky.

Outside of these cinematic adventures, Lancaster could be unforgiving. Kids were cruel, and the teachers were somehow worse. Every day after elementary school, I had to navigate home through a desolate landscape populated by older kids on bikes who'd chase me through gauntlets of tumbleweeds, off-leash junkyard dogs with anger management issues and dust storms that made me feel like I was trekking across Arrakis while being hunted by the junior varsity crew from *Deliverance*.

With precious little joy to be found in reality, films became my escape, along with comic books, fantasy novels and whatever terrible network television could offer. Our family never took a single vacation—anywhere. We couldn't afford to see the world beyond this tiny desert outpost, so I had to imagine what existed beyond the wasteland. I believe that's where my desire and ability to tell stories began: pure desperation, disguised as creativity.

This sets up the oldest question in the world of creative endeavors: Where the hell do you begin?

I was a spectacularly horrible student. Algebra might as well have been hieroglyphics, I couldn't spell my way out of a paper bag and I wanted to be anywhere but trapped in a classroom listening to adults drone about subjects that seemed designed to crush the human spirit. I ended up ditching about a quarter of my high school career, mostly to hang out at Del Taco, play video games, listen to metal and haunt the local movie theater.

I loved film so obsessively that when I turned 16, the first place I went job hunting was that same theater. I lucked out and got hired as an usher, which was like being paid to attend film school—if film school specialized in watching *Top Gun* over 200 times in one summer.

So when my junior-year English teacher announced we'd be watching Francis Ford Coppola's *Rumble Fish*, this chronic truant suddenly found religion and showed up to class.

That particular teacher also taught performing arts and proudly directed high school productions of *Oklahoma!* She considered herself something of a film connoisseur and proclaimed *Rumble Fish* one of the great cinematic achievements of our time. We watched it, dissected it and discussed camera angles and actor choices with the reverence typically reserved for religious texts. Finally, we were assigned an essay about how the film made us feel and what profound insights we'd gleaned.

For once I was excited about an assignment. After all, I worked at the movie theater five days a week, seeing the same films repeatedly, studying them and watching how audiences reacted to certain scenes. I thought I knew a thing or two about cinema. This essay would be a piece of cake, I figured. If only all assignments could tap into my expertise.

When my essay came back, I did a double take. A large red "D" was scrawled across the top like a scarlet letter of academic failure.

After class, I confronted the teacher, who explained in her slow, condescending drawl that I didn't understand the film— the subtext, the themes or the nuances that separated true cinema from mere entertainment. This was one of the few times I'd put genuine effort into a high school assignment, and I'd failed spectacularly. For context, in that same class with the same teacher, I'd received a B on an essay about *The Scarlet Letter*—a book I'd never read, basing my entire analysis on the back cover synopsis.

She made me second-guess everything I thought I knew about films. Maybe working at a theater and overdosing on the cinematic junk food of the '80s—having seen *Fright Night*, *Critters* and *Cobra* more times than any human should—hadn't prepared me to understand "true cinema" the way my theater-slash-English teacher had.

Fast-forward to college, where I encountered a screen-writing instructor who spent most of his time complaining that the creators of *Cheers* had stolen his idea. One day, he proudly screened his short film—what he considered the original *Cheers* —while perched on a stool at the front of the class. With his distended belly and mullet, he looked like Danny McBride from *Eastbound & Down* as he stared at us, cataloging our every reaction to his masterpiece.

It was spectacularly awful: unfunny, poorly acted and amateurishly written. The only thing it had in common with *Cheers* was it was set in a bar. For our first major assignment, we had to outline a screenplay. I got to work. I had a ton of ideas and wrote them all out. It was about a guy in his early 20s who starts dating a girl and finds out she's a vampire. My fresh idea was *this type of vampire doesn't drink blood—they suck up your energy and aura*. It was kind of cool. I even included song cues.

Another D. The instructor informed me that screenwriting wasn't my calling and suggested I drop the class.

I did. After all, he was a college professor and a supposed expert in screenwriting. Who was I to argue?

In my senior year of college, I took a film theory class with another instructor. One day, I asked him how to break into screenwriting. He constantly bragged about his connections in the film industry, so I hoped for some insider knowledge. Instead, he brushed me off with the enthusiasm of someone asked to explain quantum physics to a toddler: "I don't know, read some screenwriting books, I guess." He then scampered away as if my question was wasting his precious time.

Thanks to the internet, I can now look up these so-called experts who told me I had no future in screenwriting. Only one has any IMDb credits, and the pinnacle of his achievement was producing a behind-the-scenes featurette for a skateboard film in the late '80s.

What all three instructors had in common was their ability to dissect Robert Bresson's *Pickpocket* and analyze the themes of Bergman's *Persona*, but they didn't know shit about how the film business actually worked. They were like food critics who'd never worked in a kitchen, pontificating about cuisine while surviving on microwave dinners.

Ms. Rumble Fish taught high school plays until retirement. I saw the screenwriting professor years later, shit-faced in a bar and falling off his stool—a performance more compelling than anything he'd ever written. The film theory professor now owns a bed and breakfast and still calls himself a producer and director, presumably to impress guests who don't know better.

What I've learned is that there are thousands of instructors and experts who know very little to nothing about the film and television *business*. Screenwriting coaches, script doctors and coverage services—99 percent of these experts have never made a dime in the industry. There are hundreds of books on how to write scripts, but few authors have ever sold one, let alone had a film made.

What they can't tell you is how the business actually works. How do you hustle that amazing script once you've finished writing it? How do you navigate the beautiful, soul-crushing maze that transforms a 108-page document into a multi-million-dollar film?

You don't have to be Aaron Sorkin or Quentin Tarantino to write and sell screenplays. You do, however, need to work on your craft relentlessly. You should write at least five to 10 scripts before trying to get professionals to read your material. That's not a typo: *five to 10 complete screenplays.*

If you think you can write one script, sell it for a fortune and get a film made, you're either delusional or more talented than anyone I know in this business. What you don't see is that most professional screenwriters are constantly writing. I usually have 20 projects in different stages of development at any given time—some optioned, others close to financing and some just scripts circulating among producers.

If you only have one script and you're betting the farm on

it, what happens when it doesn't work out? What's your follow-up to failure?

I grew up in a wasteland populated by crystal meth cooks, petty criminals and assorted degenerates. I didn't get an MFA from an Ivy League school. I had no family connections in the film business. To this day, I still couldn't identify an adverb if it performed a song-and-dance number in front of me.

Yet I've optioned, sold or been hired on at least 50 projects. Some saw daylight; others are buried in development hell like forgotten pharaohs. But for over 20 years, writing and selling screenplays has been my only job. I found a way to make a living in this impossible business.

If a maladjusted kid from the desert can do it, so can you.

The trick is ignoring the experts and learning how the business works—not how film school professors think it should work, but how it truly operates in all its chaotic, counterintuitive glory.

CHAPTER 3

ETERNAL SUNSHINE OF THE SAMPLE SCRIPT

IT WAS A SMALL PARTY—MAYBE 20 people were there. I was sitting on a couch in the opulent living room, nursing an old-fashioned alone...until someone plopped down on the couch across from me. We locked eyes.

It was Jack Nicholson.

Jack. Fucking. Nicholson.

My mind started to race. What should I say? *Loved you in Chinatown? I'm a big fan? You were the Joker?* Every scenario I ran through had me looking like an idiot. I decided to play it cool.

I gave him a head nod.

Long BEAT.

He returned it and smiled. I realized he was just there to chill out and appreciated the fact I didn't bug him with some forgettable small talk. He was there to enjoy himself at his good friend Robert Evans' home.

Yes, that Robert Evans.

The one who, as head of Paramount, oversaw the production of *The Godfather* and *The Godfather Part II*. He produced *Chinatown* (which starred Jack Nicholson). His book *The Kid Stays in the Picture* is a must-read for anyone in the film business. Evans was down the hall from where Jack and I were perched, in his bedroom, draped in his ubiquitous pajamas and holding court.

I ended up at this small soiree because Robert Evans and his company wanted to produce the first script my writing partner and I had written.

It was called *LA Gothic*.

It was a horror anthology with a *Pulp Fiction*-like structure (maybe more like John August's *Go*), where all the divergent stories converged in the third act. One storyline focused on a vampire who was an actor in '70s horror films in his former life. Another spotlighted a demon-possessed rock star. The third took place during a drug-fueled zombie outbreak at a nightclub. At the center of it all was a single father who worked as a drug counselor by day and a vampire hunter by night. He was torn between hunting down evil while attempting to keep his teenage daughter out of trouble. It was energetic, crass and drenched in gore.

Evans loved it. So did his head of production. I can't remember her name, but I do remember that one of her notes was, "Put more of that fuckin' religious shit in there, I love that fuckin' religious shit."

Many years later, I still don't know how to address that note.

It was cool to have a legendary producer love our first script. Unfortunately, outside of going to some meetings at his old-school bungalow on the Paramount lot and being invited to that party at his house, not much else happened—so we moved on.

Our manager decided to start sending out *LA Gothic*, and executives and producers loved its non-linear structure, the off-the-wall characters and nonstop visceral violence. It opened doors for us and put us on the map as up-and-coming writers.

We were called "baby writers," a term used in the film business to let everyone know you're new to the game. Even though we were in our 30s, the name applied to us. And as baby writers, we were off and running. One afternoon, I got a call from my manager:

"John Carpenter read your script *LA Gothic*, digs it and wants to meet."

"What?" I stared at the phone, not sure what to say. On the other end, a faint "You still there?" echoed out.

I asked again, "John Carpenter? The master of horror? The guy who directed *Halloween, Escape From New York, The Thing*? The same guy who directed a big slice of the films I obsessed over growing up?"

"Yeah, he wants you to come up to his office and talk. Today."

I arrived at Carpenter's office, a Craftsman house in Hollywood right behind the Guitar Center. Carpenter turned out to be the coolest guy I'd ever met—smart, gracious, straightforward and take-no-shit.

He liked the script but wanted us to bring it to the next level. So, for the next few weeks, we'd go to his office, where we'd talk about the NBA, politics, film history and video games before getting to work on the script.

It was a masterclass in what a script needs to appeal to a director. Carpenter would go over a scene and halfway through an action line, he'd stop. He'd look at us and say, "How do I shoot this?" Other places in the script, he'd think for a beat and come back with, "Whose story is this?"

At one point in the screenplay, the lead character (who was somewhat modeled after Snake Plissken) yelled at a vampire to "shut up." Carpenter took a long beat, drolly read the line aloud: "Shut up." He looked up and said, "See how bad that sounds? Don't have your protagonist yell 'shut up.' Makes him look weak. Have him punch the motherfucker in the face—that illustrates the point." Point taken.

He went through the script line by line, beat by beat. Occasionally he'd issue a "That's good." I took it all in and appreciated every criticism. Other times Carpenter would pause while reading our script aloud and say, "You can do better."

Months—maybe years—were spent trying to get the film put together with Carpenter, but the business side never quite clicked. As cool as the script was with its highly original structure, it never got made.

One of the issues people had was that the lead of the film didn't show up in the script until page 17. One producer argued the lead needed to show up sooner. I countered with, "Luke Skywalker doesn't show up in *Star Wars* until after 10 minutes." He came back with, "If we send the script to an actor to play the lead and they don't see themselves in the story until page 17, that's not a selling point."

You know what? The producer was right. And for all my bravado about Luke Skywalker staying in the shadows until 10 minutes into the film, I later found out that in a rough cut of *Star Wars*, Luke appears in the first few scenes—but those scenes had been cut from the final edit. I was wrong on multiple fronts.

A lesson in screenwriting I keep in mind today: When you're at the script stage of a project, what makes the best read for all involved? At this stage, you're not writing for the finished product (a completed film). You're writing for producers, actors and directors who are going to read the screenplay. Your main goal is to create a script that's going to make them say, "I want to do this."

LA Gothic with Carpenter at the helm never panned out. But the work and relationship benefited in other ways:

Carpenter requested that my writing partner at the time and I do an uncredited rewrite on his next film, *The Ward*.

No credit, but a pretty good payday. The script was written by two brothers, and it was a great script, but the producers and Carpenter felt something was missing. A quick diagnosis revealed that the main character's journey was passive—things just happened to her, and she was along for the ride.

They set up a conference call to discuss how to improve the script. Several executives and producers were on the call as well as Carpenter. As we explained that what the script needed was a more active protagonist, the call was quickly hijacked by executives adding their thoughts—at one point their enthusiasm led to them all talking over each other.

Carpenter's voice cut through the line. "Guys, stop. Just go let the writers do what they do." That was it. End of notes. It was a badass move. Carpenter had earned the right to politely tell everyone involved in the project to shut the fuck up. It was amazing. I'm still waiting to get to a point in my career when I can do this.

The next day, we were hired—with a caveat. They needed the rewrite done in a week. The reason? They wanted to send it to Amber Heard immediately to play the lead and needed to get her aboard the project ASAP for the film to be financed. Challenge accepted.

We got to work on our revisions. My big addition was at the beginning of the script when we meet the lead. Instead of passively lounging around in a hospital ward, she burns down a church and is on the run from the police. It was a great way to start off a film that mostly takes place in an institution, and it immediately explained who the character was: a badass trying to escape her situation who would fight every step of the way to achieve her goals.

Carpenter loved the changes to the script—except for one.

He said, "Who added the thing with the rats?" I pointed to myself. He said, "That's just too much...plus, I don't want to work with rats."

Fair enough. The rat thing was something I'd come up with to inform the lead character's backstory (spoiler alert: she had been kidnapped as a child and tied up in the basement of a church—hence the reason she burns it down at the start of the film). This character spent several days tied up in a basement, and rats had started chewing on her feet, scarring her physically and mentally. It was brutal, but the script was about a girl who had developed multiple personalities from the trauma of this horrific experience.

The rat thing was taken out of the screenplay. Good thing, because the 12-year-old actress playing a younger version of Amber Heard's character was none other than Sydney Sweeney. Last thing I want to be known for is being the guy who came up with the idea of rats eating little Sydney Sweeney's feet.

Working with Carpenter was a boost of confidence and a masterclass in the business. He gave us lots of advice about the industry, but the one thing he emphasized more than anything else was: "Don't start writing...until they pay you." Words to live by.

LA Gothic didn't get made with Carpenter, but it didn't die either. It was optioned several more times, and we got paid each time. At this point, we've probably made at least $150,000 for a project that never got made—and we still own the rights.

LA Gothic served as an amazing sample script over and over.

What's a sample? A sample screenplay shows what you can do. It's your résumé. It demonstrates that your screenwriting skills are at a professional level. It conveys how you handle plot, pacing, character development, scene transitions and dialogue.

It's your calling card—a screenplay you or your reps can send to a producer or executive looking to hire a writer for an OWA (open writing assignment). How many samples do you need? It depends on the jobs you're trying to get. For instance, if you're up to write *John Wick 5*, a comedy sample won't cut it —you'll need an action sample. If you're focused on TV, you'll need a sample pilot.

WHAT MAKES A GREAT SAMPLE?

First of all, it has to be professional. That means it's gone through multiple rewrites, the formatting is correct, the same words or actions aren't repeated within the same scene, there are no widow words and more.

Another thing: You must grab the reader's attention in the first five pages.

Producers and studio executives can tell within a few pages if your script has what it takes to play in the big leagues. In those first five pages, you'd better introduce the setup, the main character and some conflict. Your job is to make sure whoever's reading your script keeps turning the pages and doesn't toss it aside. Ask yourself: Can you condense four pages of dialogue into one and get the same emotional point across? Can you crash a plane on page one? Can you have a massive shootout on page three?

Your screenplay's page count matters too. Screenplays should generally be between 95 and 108 pages, depending on the genre. Formatting is also crucial—look at scripts from produced films in your genre to see how it's done. How is a jump scare presented on the page? How is a violent fistfight written? A flashback?

Remember, a great read on the page might not always translate to compelling visuals, but at this stage, you only have one job: create a great read.

Every time I think *LA Gothic* is in my past, it rises again from the dead. It's proof that a great sample can keep you in the game. It was pitched as a TV show at one point with Carpenter attached to direct the pilot. We had a meeting at William Morris Agency (before they became WME). After our pitch, the lead TV literary agent in the room stated with absolute authority, "No one wants a vampire TV show." Not long after that, *True Blood, Vampire Diaries* and *The Strain* all became hits.

A few years ago, Nicolas Winding Refn heard about the project, dug the concept and wanted to try to make it into a TV show. I love Refn's work, so this was an amazing turn of events. We quickly made a deal and started meeting to discuss ideas at Refn's home once a week. As with Carpenter, it was another masterclass in filmmaking—and unbelievably, I was being paid to riff ideas and talk film with NWR. Refn is a very smart guy who also understands pop culture and knows his film history inside and out. Much like Carpenter, he intellectualizes film but also has a 1970s grindhouse sensibility.

We never got around to writing the pilot due to Refn's other obligations. We still got paid, and the rights reverted back to us—again.

A great sample script can set you up to build a career. *LA Gothic* stood out because it was weird and unusual (which is also probably why it never got made). We had many meetings with interested producers asking how we could bring down the budget to make it work financially. Despite never being made, *LA Gothic* helped open a lot of doors.

And it got me invited to a party at Robert Evans' house—with a seat directly across from Jack fucking Nicholson.

CHAPTER 4

NO COUNTRY FOR
CONTROL FREAKS

ONE TIME A PRODUCER said to me, "We should have the lead character drive a Bentley." I thought, *Really? In what universe does a police detective drive a Bentley?*

On another project, a producer suggested we add a motorcycle chase to the script. The scene as written was a modest chase between two cars—one evading the other, nothing flashy, nothing that screamed "We need a big motorcycle chase here." It didn't fit tonally with the rest of the film. Yet he was obsessed with this elaborate chase sequence.

On still another film, I was sent the first edit of the completed film to review. Suddenly, a character appeared who wasn't in the script. This character had no purpose in the story —worse, it was a caricature, the villain's blood-licking female sidekick who couldn't act and gave a simultaneously wooden yet overacted performance that defied the laws of physics.

The explanation for all these terrible creative decisions is the same: They weren't made for the good of the film. They were made for the good of a producer or financier.

I later discovered that if we put a Bentley in the film, the producer who suggested it could get 50 percent off a Bentley he coveted. In the case of the motorcycle chase, it was the same scenario—if we inserted a certain brand of motorcycle into the film, the producer would receive several free bikes. The hacky blood-licking sidekick? One of the producers' girlfriends, naturally.

You've spent months, maybe years, perfecting your script. Every word of dialogue is dynamic, every scene flows with beginning, middle and end. The plot is executed to perfection; the second act turn surprises everyone. You get it out to producers, executives and filmmakers. They love it, they lavish you with praise, they want to option it and even pay you a small amount of money for that privilege.

Brace yourself, because what comes next are changes to your perfectly crafted script. Can they do that? *Yes.* Can they do that without your input? *Absolutely.* Will it make the script better or worse? *That's* the million-dollar question.

Why would anyone want to option your amazing script and then butcher it? A producer might think changes are needed to make it more appealing, more commercial or edgier. An actor may like the concept but need to "connect on a deeper level" with their character, which usually means making the character more like themselves. A financier may want to make it more like whatever successful film just came out.

Once your script is actually purchased, the situation becomes even more dire. They no longer need you to make changes or even consult you about them. You've exchanged money for control of your script. Someone else owns it now, like they own their car or their coffee table.

You can diplomatically try to guide the project and preserve your vision, but you're no longer the captain of your creative ship. The trade-off is that you've made money for writing a screenplay and hopefully a film is being made from it. If they want to change your male lead to a female character, they can do that. If they want the villain to survive the ending you crafted so carefully, they can do that too.

Think of it like selling anything else—a house, for example. Once you cash that check and sign those papers, the new owner can paint it pink, install Astroturf in the living room or turn it into a combination Taco Bell and nail salon. It's theirs to do with as they please. All you can do is hope their vision doesn't completely desecrate yours.

This is why maintaining a positive relationship with whoever options your script is crucial. You've essentially given them creative control, and if you're not on the same page, your only recourse is waiting for the option to expire, getting your script back and praying you're smart enough not to make the same mistake twice.

It takes an army to make a film: actors, directors, producers, financiers, studio executives, editors, cinematographers and dozens of others. What you imagined while writing will almost certainly not match the finished product. It might be better than you dreamed, it might be completely different or it might be an unrecognizable disaster that makes you question every life choice that led you to this moment.

You have to surrender control of your script when it becomes a film. If you can't handle that reality—if you need to maintain complete creative authority over your vision, then you should probably write novels instead. At least when you write a book, the only person who can ruin it is you.

This is the beautiful, soul-crushing reality of screenwriting: your script is a product, not a sacred text. The sooner you accept that, the better equipped you'll be to navigate the gorgeous nightmare that is getting your work produced.

CHAPTER 5

PITCH NOT SO PERFECT

SO YOU'VE WRITTEN a couple of scripts that have gained some traction in the film business. Congratulations. You're now eligible for what they call OWAs—open writing assignments.

Here's how the dance works: You sit across from producers, executives or other varieties of Hollywood vagrants who've optioned some book, comic or half-remembered fever dream. They need a writer. You need money. It's a beautiful, dysfunctional relationship waiting to happen.

Many times, they'll send you some form of IP—a comic book, a novel or a foreign film—for you to digest before the meeting.

Then, after you spend a week or so reading, thinking, writing and rewriting your vision for the material, you go in person (or on Zoom) to lay out your vision for their IP—for the next Marvel tentpole or prestige HBO limited series.

And you pitch your *take* on the material.

A take is essentially an audition disguised as a creative exercise—a performance wrapped in a book report. To be clear, it's a lot of work to prepare a take. I'd argue it's possibly more work than auditioning for a part as an actor.

Do most writers have to do this? Of course we fucking do.

The only writers who skip this ritual are the ones with track records who live in the rarified air of the top one percent of screenwriters. The rest of us— the working population—get to dance like trained seals.

Here's what I've learned after years of this ritual: You want to nail down the big picture—plot points, themes and characters—without giving away too much. You don't need to cover every plot point and character arc. Show them you're passionate about their baby and that you understand what makes it tick. But don't be too specific. Never give them a reason to say no.

The golden rule of takes? Leave them wanting more, not checking their phones and wondering if they can make their lunch reservation.

One of the first big swings I took was for the comic book *Scott Pilgrim vs. the World*. This was before Edgar Wright got his talented hands on it.

They sent over the comics. I devoured them, spending every waking moment coming up with plot points and character development. Two weeks later, it was all mapped out: an 18-page take that covered every beat, arc and action sequence in detail. On the big pitch day, the conference room was filled with producers and executives. My then-writing partner and I read it to them. Every. Single. Word.

For over an hour.

Picture this: a room full of executives slowly dying inside while a crew of baby writers methodically explain how they'd "fix" their property. Their eyes glazed over. In hindsight, the excitement I thought I felt in the room was actually tension that read: "Let's get this the fuck over with." I left thinking it had been a demonstration of creative genius.

We didn't get the job. They never even called our agent back to let him know we didn't get the job. We'd just been ghosted by a room full of A-list producers and studio executives.

Lesson learned: Executives don't want you to have it all figured out or read every beat to them. They want to leave their own mark. They want to feel like collaborators, not checkbook-wielding spectators. It's their project, their vision and you're just the cook they've hired to prepare it. Don't forget that, even when—especially when—you know you could do it better with both hands tied behind your back.

Years later, we were up for a James Patterson adaptation for a TV pilot. Instead of the verbose display we'd inflicted on the *Scott Pilgrim* team, we went minimal: a brief outline of the pilot and show structure. Clean, simple, leaving room for their input. It was basically an under-pitch.

We got the job.

It was a great concept, solid IP and amazing executives. But like most pilots, it was a baby sea turtle that never made it to the shore. That's the cruel arithmetic of this business: For every show that gets made, a thousand die in development hell, picked apart by notes and network politics until there's nothing left but a pile of revised drafts and broken dreams.

Right after the first *Iron Man* hit theaters, we found ourselves in a meeting at Marvel Entertainment. This was back when they were still hungry, before they became the cultural Death Star they are today. They asked if we had any ideas for Marvel IP.

We pitched a show about the gangs of New York centered on Marvel characters. It featured a young Kingpin clawing his way to power while battling the Maggia, AIM and every other Marvel criminal organization with a foothold in NYC. We threw in B- and C-list characters like Whiplash and Boomerang —having no idea Whiplash would show up in *Iron Man* 2.

They liked the idea, but at the time they had no TV department.

Then there was my Luke Cage pitch (another Marvel character). I kept it simple, almost conversational.

Picture this: 1977. Young Luke Cage is broke with no prospects. To support his young family, he joins a gang. He gets busted and sentenced to 20 years. To get out early and see his son, he volunteers for an experimental program. He dies in the experiment and gets buried in the prison graveyard.

Cut to today: Cage digs himself out of the ground. The experiment rebuilt his cells over two decades—he never died; he was just in suspended animation. He talks like it's still the '70s, using his catchphrases from the comic book. He's a man out of time with superhuman strength—and a son who's now a decorated NYPD detective. The son became a cop specifically to avoid being like his criminal father.

The son's working a case against the corrupt mayor. Luke wants to reconcile, but before he can reveal who he is, his son explains what a piece of shit his father was. That night the son gets killed by the mayor's goons. Luke takes on his son's mission, using his powers to take down the mayor and his rogue's gallery of criminals. He makes the city a better place for everyone.

Themes: fathers and sons, redemption and making good on past mistakes. At the end, Luke takes on his son's cause and becomes Hero for Hire—helping those who need help and can't find it.

In three minutes, I covered plot, character motivation, themes and honored the source material while making it contemporary. That's what a good pitch does—it's a perfect little ecosystem that makes sense on its own terms.

Want to know the most soul-crushing part? Sometimes you have the best take and still don't get the job. I've had executives tell me years later, "You had the best pitch, but we had to hire someone with a bigger résumé."

That's the game. You can't get angry about it. I understand their position. If they hire me and I turn in a great pilot that doesn't get made, they look bad for taking a chance on the less experienced writer. If they hire some A-list writer, pay them a fortune and the show still dies, well—that's just market forces. They hired the best person available. Perfect cover.

This is why we have so many terrible remakes and sequels. It's not that Hollywood lacks creativity—it's that creativity is dangerous. Safer to hire the proven name to adapt *Underworld 5* than to gamble on the unknown writer with the brilliant original idea (and yes, we did a pitch for *Underworld 5*, which ended up being called *Blood Wars*).

Sometimes, you have to pitch projects you don't like, don't understand or actively hate. But you want the job because it pays well—and that's what working-class screenwriters do: We work. You take every gig you can get because they're few and far between, and pride doesn't pay the rent. Other times you get to pitch dream projects. I once helped craft a pitch for a *Black Hole* remake, as well as a TV show based on one of my favorite DC Comics characters, Warlord.

The rules change when you're pitching your own material. If you're up for an action film and you've got a great action script as a sample, you can walk in and give a 10-minute pitch on your next project. If they love it and trust your sample, you might get hired on the spot.

But more often, even if they love the pitch, they still need to show it to their boss. That's when you send over a few pages reiterating what you pitched. Same rules apply: cover plot, characters and themes. Get in, get out and leave a good impression. Think of it like a first date—you want them excited to see you again, not checking their watch.

The strangest thing about pitches is that they either work or they don't—and you can usually tell within the first few sentences. After a few years, I developed a sixth sense for when an executive was into a pitch and when he was already planning what to order at Nobu later that night.

This matters because if they're not vibing with your four-sentence elevator pitch, they're sure as hell not going to be into the detailed version or the actual script. There are a thousand reasons why they might not be interested: It's not their thing, it's not what their company is looking for or they already have something similar in development. That last one happens more than you'd think—great minds think alike, and terrible minds think in focus groups.

I once ran into a producer friend at a coffee shop who asked what I was working on. I told her about a zombie film idea I had where you're immune to a virus as long as you're still growing, but once you hit around 18 you become infected. The virus is airborne, so you're left with a world of teenagers (and young kids) trying to survive while being, well, teenagers. They're just as concerned with racing through the apocalypse in stolen Range Rovers and getting laid as they are with finding a cure. It was *Return of the Living Dead* meets John Hughes.

She said, "Love it; call you later today."

Two weeks later, we had a director attached and a company paying us to write the script. It was that easy. It was the right pitch at the right time. It turned out to be another cool project that got stuck in development hell—but the pitch worked because it was easy to understand. You could envision the trailer, the poster and the casting.

This is why you need multiple pitches and the ability to pivot fast. In every general meeting—and I've been in hundreds —you'll be asked what you're working on. If you start with your best idea and they fire back, "We've got something like that," you need to pivot immediately to idea number two, then three.

If idea number three is half-baked, you bullshit with enthusiasm. If they get excited about that one, you say, "Still have a few kinks to work out, but it's cool—you're gonna love it. I'll send you a pitch document in a day or two."

Then you go home and figure that half-idea out. You write and rewrite it and think about it and think about it.

All in the hope that, at the end, you might actually get paid to write.

CHAPTER 6
SOME RISKY BUSINESS

WHEN I first decided to focus primarily on screenwriting, I would take any job for any amount. Quick rewrites on action scripts for $500 here, a grand there. A lot of work for embarrassingly little money, but as the old saying goes, you're not truly a professional until someone's paying you.

I call these quick fixes (work for no credit and little pay) "script pimping."

In the late '90s and early 2000s, DJing at a trashy Hollywood bar every Friday night paid my bills, leaving my days free to focus on one thing: becoming a working screenwriter—or at least one who could afford to buy groceries without checking his account balance first.

One afternoon, a producer who had sporadically paid me to do quick rewrites summoned me to his production office on Sunset Boulevard. And yes, he really used the word "summoned" when he called; that should have been my first warning sign. When I arrived, he told me to take a seat. I sank into the chair across from his desk while he sat up straight, looked me dead in the eye and delivered his pitch with the confidence of a man who genuinely believed he was about to change my life.

"I got a gig for you. You're gonna write this film and I'm going to produce it."

I figured it was another low-level action film, probably a Steven Seagal vehicle where someone's daughter gets kidnapped in Eastern Europe and justice is served via broken necks and one-liners.

He skipped the creative preamble entirely and went straight to the business end. "I can get you paid $300,000. Maybe more."

I sat up. That grabbed my attention. My head instantly started spinning. *Three hundred grand? You know what you could do with that kind of money? That's a down payment on a house—if you're willing to buy somewhere outside LA where people actually have lawns. I could pay off all my credit cards. Buy a car that doesn't sound like it's dying every time I turn the ignition.*

"It's a biopic," he continued. "About this guy and his life story. His son wants to get into the film business, make a film about his father, and they need a screenwriter. You'd be perfect."

I'm thinking: *Amazing. Who the fuck is this guy? Some forgotten silent film star? A jazz musician? A war hero?*

And then he said it.

"Gaddafi."

Pause.

"As in Muammar Gaddafi?" I asked, certain I'd misheard.

"Yeah, Gaddafi," he replied, calm as someone ordering a sandwich. "Muammar Gaddafi. The leader of Libya."

"The terrorist who blew up a plane over Scotland that killed 270 people?" I asked, just to be absolutely clear we were talking about the same mass-murdering dictator.

"Yeah, but look—they want to make a film about his story, rehabilitate his image."

He could see on my face that I wasn't exactly bursting with enthusiasm.

"I don't know," I shot back.

He shifted into high gear, amping up his pitch like a used car salesman who sensed the deal slipping away. "Come on, they'll send a plane to pick us up and take us to Libya to meet with him. One of those pimped-out 767 luxury jets. And when we get there, they'll take us to a tent in the middle of the desert where they throw these crazy parties that last for days—tons of hot chicks, the whole thing. It'll be an adventure!"

An adventure. *Right. Like getting kidnapped is an adventure. Like becoming an international propaganda tool is an adventure.*

I told him I'd think about it. As I was leaving, he yelled after me, "They have tons of cash! Might be able to get you $350,000!"

By the time I walked up Sunset to my apartment a few blocks away, I'd made my decision. No fucking way was I getting involved with a terrorist. Not my style. I'd rather be a broke writer with a functional conscience than a well-paid one wondering if I'd end up on a watchlist somewhere.

They never made that film about Gaddafi. A few years later, he was killed by his own people in a revolt, his dead body paraded through the streets. I'd like to think I dodged more than just a bullet on that one—more like an entire firing squad.

A few years later, I was working on a screenplay for a real estate developer. His pitch: He had a "crazy story" and wanted to turn it into a film. A vanity project. By this point, I was an established writer with exactly zero interest in writing propaganda pieces about boring rich guys who thought their lives warranted cinematic treatment.

So I threw out a huge fee, the kind of number designed to make someone go away.

He bit.

As I started learning about his backstory, I discovered he'd spent time in federal prison for selling over 100 helicopters to North Korea in the '80s—a time when selling military equipment to communist countries was a big no-no. Like, international-incident-level no-no.

He explained that he was innocent, that it was all a mix-up and that the screenplay and film would set the record straight. Clear his name. Justice would finally be served.

I shrugged. "Not sure how over 100 helicopters get misplaced in the wrong country, but okay." After all, he was paying for it.

Nothing ever happened with that story. I made some money. No harm, no foul. Well, except for the 100 helicopters that ended up in North Korea, but that wasn't technically my problem.

I continued for many years doing quick fixes on scripts. Mostly through networking and word of mouth. *Hellraiser 10?* I did a quick fix on that. *Urban Explorer?* Yup, that one too.

A few years later, my writing partner and I were approached about doing a rewrite on an action screenplay that had a young, up-and-coming star attached. I read the script—it was horrible. Yet it was a studio project, so I was down with getting paid to fix it.

After a call with the executive in charge, the story of why this thing was such a piece of shit became clear. The young action star's manager (who also happened to be his father) had signed off on the first act and loved it. The studio needed someone to fix the screenplay (which they knew was bad) without touching the first 25 pages.

This was pretty much impossible, since the entire foundation of the screenplay—the first act—established an unlikable asshole in unbelievable, ridiculous situations that somehow gave him nano-bot powers and he became a hero. Eventually, they came to their senses and decided to shelve the project before hiring any more writers to bang their head against the wall to make it work.

Another reason bad films get made: tiptoeing around talent and what they like instead of having a frank conversation with them. Everyone's too afraid to say it sucks because the actor (the one who's truly getting the film financed) might walk.

I've been as guilty of doing this as these execs were. Sometimes you'll just shut up instead of fight because you need a payday.

Antoine Fuqua—the guy who directed blockbusters like *Training Day* and *The Equalizer*—optioned our screenplay *Tokarev* (later released as *Rage*) with plans to direct. He ended up getting busy with other projects and never made the film, but he did hook us up with a writing gig for something he was producing.

The project centered on the LAPD's Special Investigation Section—a 20-man squad known as the most badass cops in the LAPD, possibly the world. These guys trained with Delta Force and Navy SEALs just to keep their skills sharp. They weren't your average traffic cops.

Fuqua told us he first learned about SIS while shooting *Training Day*. They'd filmed in some legitimately dangerous neighborhoods, and whenever one of the SIS members showed up, the whole vibe shifted. These guys wore plainclothes and matching belt buckles, and they struck fear into the toughest neighborhoods in Los Angeles. That's a very specific kind of reputation.

Fuqua wanted to produce a gritty, realistic film about SIS and their members. So he arranged for two retired SIS guys— who between them had been in over 50 gunfights during their careers—to take us around the seedy parts of LA and show us where they used to operate.

They drove us through South Central, then we entered the Imperial Courts housing project. Four white guys in an SUV. We stuck out like missionaries at a strip club.

As we cruised through the neighborhood, they pointed out various locations where they'd either apprehended or shot someone. Just casual tour guide stuff: "That's where I collared a guy with three kilos. That corner's where I shot a gang member who pulled on my partner."

A crew of gangsters noticed us and started heading our way. Within a millisecond, both retired SIS guys had their guns at their sides inside the SUV, ready for action. They told us to stay cool—no sudden movements—as they slowly drove through what felt like a very tense gauntlet.

For a moment, I was living a scene from *Training Day*. Except this wasn't a movie set. This was real. And I was suddenly very aware that my skill set—typing words on a computer—was completely fucking useless in this situation.

We made it out unscathed. Over the following weeks, we had more ride-alongs and lunches at run-down Chinese restaurants while they showed us their perspective of LA, regaling us with insane stories of cops and criminals, the kind of tales that made you wonder how any of them survived to retirement.

We wrote a great script. But like so many other projects, it disappeared into the Hollywood ether.

That's the thing about this business: Sometimes the best stories are the ones that never get made—the ones that exist only in draft form, in pitch meetings or in the memories of writers who got paid to live briefly in someone else's dangerous, fascinating world.

CHAPTER 7

FINAL MISSED DESTINATION

THE CALL WENT OUT: "Stop the actors from getting on the plane." I'm not sure who in the production office made the call, but they were frantic. Several actors were scheduled to fly out that morning to start filming a screenplay I co-wrote, titled *Damned*.

Damned was a twisted tale about a family on a private jet that crashes in the middle of nowhere during a snowstorm. They're taken in by a clan of backwoods survivalists who believe the End of Days is nigh, and the family falling out of the sky is the ultimate sign. It was like *Misery*, but with a whole family—stranded, injured and without help. They had to rely on their wits and inner strength to survive.

As a follow-up to *LA Gothic*, it was a hit within the circle of producers and executives that read it. Everyone saw its potential as a deeply messed-up horror film that made a few sly digs at society and religion. It didn't take sides—there were no good guys or bad guys, just differing perspectives and a hell of a lot of horrific moments.

The script garnered a lot of interest, not only because it had great characters and a horrifying premise but because it had one other crucial thing going for it: It was basically a one-location film.

A friend of mine was working with a big-time producer who had a knack for getting films made. He read the script, loved it, and said, "Let's do it. I can get the financing." We were off. They quickly hired a British music video director to helm the project. He was enthusiastic, had great ideas and—most importantly—got the script and didn't want to change much.

They found a financier, and in a few weeks we'd be shooting in Missouri. Everything was going smoothly.

Almost every actor who read the script was into it. We even had interest from some up-and-coming actors like Lena Headey and a guy named Bradley Cooper. This was pre-*Game of Thrones* Lena Headey and pre-*Hangover* Bradley Cooper. We had no clue who either of them were and had to hunch over a laptop in the production office looking them up on IMDb.

The producer and director didn't hire either of those options (you never know who's going to be the next big thing). They cast a group of well-respected working actors. This was a small indie film and didn't need movie stars to get financed. Our money guy was all in: "Go make a good film," he said with confidence and full support.

There was an announcement in the trades about the project. That morning, the phone rang off the hook from various agencies that wanted to represent us—and why not? We had a go-film that, thanks to the press, everyone in the business now knew about.

Things were moving fast and smoothly—in hindsight, too smoothly. The producers hired the crew; the director set up shop in Missouri. The art department drafted designs for the creepy home where most of the story took place. Everything was a go.

A few days before we were set to start filming, it happened.

On the front page of *The Hollywood Reporter* (and in several other publications like *The New York Times*), the story broke. The company that was going to finance the film was broke. I mean, $50 million in debt broke. No money. No film. We were screwed.

The production office scrambled to call everyone who was flying out over the next 24 hours to tell them not to get on the plane. The film, for all intents and purposes, was dead. Ironic that a film about a family and a plane crash ended by stopping actors from getting on an actual plane.

It's completely soul-crushing to see your project get so close to being made and watch it all slip away in one day. More than a year's worth of work—writing the script, rewriting the script, going to meetings, talking with producers and directors—went up in flames in one day.

The producers ran through other options, but it was too late. Turns out that naming it *Damned* made it a self-fulfilling prophecy.

I still get asked about that script, and recently there have been some rumblings about it getting made.

CHAPTER 8
A FISTFUL OF NO DOLLARS

A FEW YEARS AGO, I was producing an indie film with a $2.5 million budget, and we set up our production offices in a shitty neighborhood at the far end of the Valley. We chose this particular shithole for strategic reasons: Every time someone visited the office, they'd think, "These guys don't have much money," which worked beautifully and gave us the leverage to make great deals with vendors, crew and actors.

Shooting a film in LA is as expensive as a cocaine habit, so we needed every dime we could save. The last thing you ever want to do when producing is spend money on an ostentatious office. Plead poverty from day one, or else people will solve every problem that arises by asking you for more money instead of using ingenuity.

One afternoon, the line producer and I walked down the street to a run-down hot dog stand for lunch. Once there, I realized I'd forgotten my wallet. Jokingly, I made a deal with the line producer: If he bought me lunch, I'd give him my five percent backend on the film. He agreed, and we even signed a napkin to make it official.

You know who made the better deal? I did.

The film made a profit, but none of it reached my pocket.

That lunch consisting of kraut dogs and chili cheese fries is the most I've ever made in backend on over 15 films where I had a piece of the profits.

How in the world does this happen? Getting paid profits on a film is like going to war—there are a million ways that backend won't reach your pocket. Fuzzy math, placement in the waterfall (a method for distributing profits), union fees, sales agent fees and deferments. It goes on and on, like a Kafka novel written by accountants.

As a writer, there are other things you can do to protect yourself financially, though "protect" might be too strong a word. "Minimize the damage" is more accurate.

The good news is you will get paid for the agreed-upon option and purchase agreement you signed. Without a clean chain of title showing that the script owner has been paid in full, there's no way the producers can sell the completed film. Those same producers might stiff the camera operator and the head wardrobe person out of a few weeks' pay and still make a sale, but without paying the writer in full, they're screwed.

While this isn't legal advice—and you should always hire an attorney, preferably one who understands the beautiful brutality of this business—here are a few things I've learned through expensive experience.

Almost always, you'll be offered backend. You hear stories about small indie films that make tons of money, but those are about as common as unicorns with accounting degrees. Take whatever backend they're offering, but instead of using up your negotiating power trying to turn a five percent backend into 7.5 percent, there are several other things you should be angling for.

Here's the first kick in the teeth: The backend you get is usually stated as a percentage of producer profits. Producer profits are defined as only 50 percent of all profits, so even if you're receiving five percent backend, it's really 2.5 percent. Congratulations, you just got screwed on this deal and didn't even know it.

If you're not in the WGA, that means no residuals. You also won't get underlying rights or separated rights. Without diving too deep into this particular circle of hell, what you should ask for in your contract is some form of payment for all sequels—not just one, but all of them—remakes, TV adaptations and all other media.

Another thing to watch for is when the copyright of your script transfers to the production company. It should never transfer until you've been paid the purchase price. Not the option price—the purchase price.

Industry standard for purchase price payment is the first day of principal photography. Once this is paid, the production company owns your script because they paid for it. This is when the copyright transfers to them. Not a moment sooner.

Another thing to scrutinize is whether your option payment is applicable to the purchase price. Let's say you were paid a $5,000 option. If the purchase price is $25,000, the production can subtract the $5,000 you've already received, leaving you with only $20,000. You should always ask that it's not applicable—they may say no, and you might have no other options, but you should always ask.

Unless you're in the WGA and they're protecting your credit, this is where things get dicey. If your contract states that you receive writing credit, the producers have to honor it. However, what they *can* do is add additional writers—maybe some who didn't do any actual work on the script—and dilute your credit.

This happened to me on the Wesley Snipes film I wrote. I wasn't in the WGA at the time, so the producer's girlfriend was given co-writing credit. There was nothing I could do about it.

You can try to add in your contract that no one can receive credit next to you unless the producers can prove that the other writers contributed at least 50 percent of the final shooting script. Does that work? Maybe—at least it offers you some protection. The last thing you want is to get your first script made, only to see four other writers you've never met listed in the credits. It happens more often than food poisoning at a gas station sushi bar.

This goes back to what I said earlier: If you can, hire an entertainment attorney. Not just any attorney, but an entertainment attorney who knows how this business actually works. It doesn't have to be a $700-an-hour lawyer who represents A-list writers. There are plenty of experienced entertainment attorneys who can help you navigate these shark-infested waters without bleeding out financially.

Think of it as insurance against your own optimism. Because in Hollywood, five percent of nothing is still nothing.

CHAPTER 9

DEEP RED FLAGS

THERE'S no feeling quite like watching your screenplay transform into an actual film. You come up with an idea in your head, then months or years later you're standing on a set with hundreds of people working to make your vision a reality.

It's a total trip.

One rain-soaked evening—a meteorological miracle in Los Angeles—I wandered down to Tower Video. It was the bastard stepchild of Tower Records, may it rest in peace alongside all the other casualties of our digital apocalypse.

Their foreign film section was a shrine to cinematic pretension, and that night, fate handed me a DVD of *The Bird with the Crystal Plumage,* Dario Argento's 1971 masterpiece—a film that would spawn a thousand film school dissertations and inspire John Carpenter to become the master of dread we know today. I'd seen it before, but not with the reverence it deserved.

That night, transfixed by the screen, I watched this symphony of blood and Technicolor unfold. The black-gloved killer. The baroque violence. The sheer audacity of it all. Lightning struck: Someone needed to write a retro Argento film. That someone, I decided with the hubris that only comes from living in Los Angeles, was me.

For those blissfully unaware, Dario Argento is the Italian filmmaker who took horror cinema and slapped it around until it confessed its deepest secrets. His "giallo" films—those stylized Italian thrillers that make American horror look like a Sunday school picnic—fundamentally rewrote the rules of cinematic terror. Directors like Carpenter, del Toro and Refn still genuflect at his altar.

My writing partner and I attacked this project with the fervor of true believers. We loaded it with every Argento trope we could remember: beautiful women in peril, amateur detectives stumbling through mysteries and unreliable cops with their own agendas. We called it *A Yellow Wolf in a Glass Coffin* —because nothing says "1970s Italian horror" quite like a title that sounds like a rejected David Bowie song.

A few weeks later, we'd finished our masterpiece, and in a rare moment of clarity, we shortened the title to *Yellow*. Not only a nod to the giallo tradition, but also a crucial plot element. We were geniuses, obviously.

I began pitching *Yellow* to every producer who'd return my calls. Most didn't get it. But one producer—a European who understood what we were attempting—passed it to a friend in Italy. That friend, through the kind of cosmic alignment that only happens in Hollywood fever dreams, knew Dario Argento personally.

A few days later, my phone rang. Rome calling. It was Dario Argento himself.

"I like the script," Argento said in his charmingly broken English. "Let's make the movie."

What the actual fuck had just happened? Weeks earlier, this script existed only in our delusional minds, and now the master himself wanted to direct it. This was either destiny or the universe's idea of a practical joke.

I was a fucking genius. Or so I thought.

We quickly found financing contingent on casting, and discovered that Argento possessed something rare in Hollywood: genuine admirers who actually wanted to work with him. Ray Liotta signed on as the detective, Asia Argento would play our female lead and Vincent Gallo was in talks to play the killer. It was a perfect storm of talent and Italian cinema credibility.

And then, as if scripted by the gods of dramatic irony, everything fell apart. Liotta had "issues." Asia became pregnant. Gallo...well, Vincent Gallo happened, whatever that means. Back to square one, with the bitter taste of almost-success still fresh.

We rebuilt with Academy Award-winner Adrien Brody as our lead, along with Emmanuelle Seigner, Roman Polanski's wife and a formidable actress in her own right, and Elsa Pataky.

I arrived in Torino, alone with my bag filled with clothes and copies of the script. A few hours later I found myself at dinner sitting across from Dario Argento himself. He was gracious, respectful and knew everything about film. I looked around this modest restaurant, thinking: *How the hell did I get here?* I was being paid to make my first film, to live in Italy for three months on someone else's dime and to work with a legend.

A few weeks into filming, everything looked fantastic. Dario even asked me to shoot second unit—an honor that felt like being knighted by the Pope of Horror. I was given a small crew and a list of shots to capture. The fact that I spoke no Italian and my crew spoke no English proved surprisingly irrelevant. Visual storytelling, it turns out, is truly universal.

Everything was proceeding according to plan until we reached the halfway point of our shooting schedule.

One of our investors vanished, taking 20 percent of our budget with him. We were halfway through production and suddenly facing shutdown. That's when Adrien Brody did something I'd never seen before in this industry: He volunteered to put a substantial portion of his own salary back into the production. Not because he had to, but because he cared more about the crew getting paid and the film getting finished than his own paycheck.

It was the classiest move I've ever witnessed in the film business.

After we wrapped, the Italians threw the kind of party that makes American wrap parties look like corporate team-building exercises. The entire cast and crew packed into a small restaurant that was apparently Turin's hottest spot. There was drinking, embracing and tears—the whole emotional spectrum of people who'd just survived something together.

The festivities moved to a bar down the street. I'd become fast friends with Patrick O, Adrien Brody's stand-in and stunt double. We were the token Americans in a crew of over a hundred, and isolation breeds solidarity. We stayed late, partied with the locals and at some point either got in a fight with bouncers or each other—my memory remains diplomatically hazy on this point.

What I do remember is being ejected through a patio window and landing on cobblestones beside the river. Our response? Find another bar, obviously. Somehow, we met some women who knew crew members, and the next thing I knew, we were drinking at their apartment somewhere in the city.

We woke up around 3 pm the next day with hangovers that felt like divine punishment. When we finally returned to our hotel, the manager was in full panic mode. "Everyone from the film is looking for you," he said. "We've had dozens of calls."

Shit. We must have done something truly horrible.

Turns out, when we were launched through that window, Patrick had left his travel bag behind. Someone rifled through it, took anything valuable and tossed the rest down the river-bank. A good Samaritan found Patrick's passport and, reasonably assuming two drunk Americans had fallen into the river and drowned, called the police.

While we were passed out at the lovely apartment of those very gracious Italian women, the police had notified the State Department representative, who called the production office. This was back when cell phones were useless overseas, so for an entire day no one could reach us and everyone assumed the worst.

We cleared everything up, and I figured the chaos was over. I could finally get on a plane back to the States.

That was until I got hit with a €5,000 hotel bill.

During post-production, *Yellow* became *Giallo*—not for any artistic reason, but because our sales agent had another film called *Yellow* and wanted to avoid confusion in the paperwork. This is how major creative decisions get made in the film industry, folks: Billing efficiency trumps artistic vision every time.

I hated the title then and still do. We suggested *The Color of Fear*, which was marginally better—not great, but not awful. The producers stuck with *Giallo* because apparently, mediocrity is a hill worth dying on.

Before the film's release, Adrien Brody filed a lawsuit. The broad strokes: When he'd bailed out the production, they'd promised to try to pay him back some of his deferred salary. Of course, they never did. They eventually coughed up some money and settled. These were the same producers who'd stiffed me with that hotel bill in Turin. Total schmucks doesn't begin to cover it.

The lesson? Even the best-laid plans can go spectacularly wrong. Dreams can transform into nightmares faster than you can say "creative differences." I got my first film made—but at what cost? I don't think anyone was creatively satisfied with the end result, and a lot of bad blood was spilled along the way.

But I did get to work alongside Dario Argento for three months—sharing dinners, sitting on set, talking film and even attending morning mass with him once. He taught me how to run a set, how to handle actors and most importantly, how to deal with producers.

The most valuable lesson of all? If you want a career as a writer, you need to develop amnesia about each project. When they're finished, you reset and start all over again. It's the only way to survive.

To this day, I've only seen *Giallo* once—at a screening before its release. I've never watched it since. I think it's because the memories I have from making that film are more dramatic than the actual film itself.

Over the years, the film has been nearly impossible to find due to the lawsuit and general mismanagement by the producers. I recently saw that it's back on several streaming platforms —with a new title: *The Color of Fear*.

My thoughts on the name change: It wasn't a creative decision. It was done to screw someone, somewhere out of some money.

CHAPTER 10
APOCALYPSE OF NOTES

EVERYONE HAS an opinion about your script. And I mean everyone.

I've been on film sets where the production designer, the stunt coordinator and even some 22-year-old production assistant three weeks into their first industry job will confidently offer up suggestions for plot points and dialogue. It's like being a chef in a kitchen where every busboy tells you how to improve your signature dish.

Everyone thinks they can do what you do: write your script —or better yet, write a superior one. In Hollywood, everyone's a screenwriter. And I mean everyone.

Here's the beautiful irony you need to cling to like a life raft in rough seas: The film is getting made because you wrote it. Not the production designer with opinions. Not the PA with fresh film school theories. You. Always remember that you know what makes your script work and why it appealed to readers in the first place. You understand its DNA in ways others can only guess at.

But then comes the inevitable moment when that same producer who lavished praise on your script to secure the option suddenly starts wanting to make changes. The very person who told you it was perfect now has a laundry list of suggestions. What do you do when the hand that feeds you starts trying to rewrite your meal?

These notes you'll inevitably receive—are they right? Does your script really need additional scenes, fewer characters and a faster second act? Are they brilliant insights that will elevate your work, or are they the worst suggestions you've ever heard from people who fundamentally misunderstand what you've created?

The truth is probably somewhere in between, which is the most maddening answer possible.

Filmmaking is a collaborative endeavor, and I like to think of it as a bunch of people who've signed on to the same pirate ship. They all have the same destination in mind—success, adoration and money—but each one wants to take a different route to get there. Some want to sail around the storm; others want to sail straight through it. The navigator thinks he knows better than the captain, and the cook is convinced the whole crew is steering toward the rocks.

Here's the one major rule that trumps all creative considerations: Unless you're working with Scorsese or Tarantino, creatives who've earned the right to call the shots through decades of success—whoever pays the bills gets the final say on all things creative, including your script.

But that's not always a catastrophe. You need to prepare yourself mentally for this reality and ask the right question: How do you get your film made while preserving the integrity of your script?

Many times, I've received notes like "I don't feel for the character," or "I don't know if this character would really do this." What they're actually saying is that they have a problem with something, but they can't articulate exactly what it is. Producers and executives are often juggling a dozen scripts simultaneously, and sometimes a piece of dialogue or a plot point just isn't landing for them. They feel something's off, but they're pointing at the wrong thing.

This is where you become a detective. You know your screenplay better than anyone else in the room, so you need to diagnose these notes and figure out what they're really saying. Is the character truly not eliciting the right emotional response, or do they just hate that monologue on page 36? Are they having a structural problem with your second act, or are they just uncomfortable with the moral ambiguity of your protagonist?

Here's where your ego either helps or destroys you. You can approach notes with the attitude of a precious artist whose vision is being corrupted by philistines—or you can see them as an opportunity to make your script bulletproof. The former approach leads to unemployment; the latter leads to produced films.

Give them wins. Make the collaboration feel real. No producer wants to buy your script, put money behind it and not leave their own fingerprints on the project. They need to feel like they've contributed something meaningful, that they're not just writing checks for someone else's vision.

This doesn't mean you have to accept every note, but it does mean you need to be strategic about which battles you fight. Pick the hills you're willing to die on, because you probably only get one or two of them.

When someone gives you a note that misses the mark, don't just dismiss it. Try to understand what problem they're trying to solve, then offer a solution that addresses their concern while preserving what you know works. It's like being a translator between their instincts and your expertise.

Remember: They're not trying to ruin your script out of malice. They're trying to make it better according to their understanding of what works. Sometimes they're right. Sometimes they're spectacularly wrong. Your job is to tell the difference and navigate accordingly.

The trick is maintaining enough flexibility to incorporate good ideas while having enough backbone to protect the core of what makes your script special. It's a delicate balance—like performing surgery while riding a unicycle.

But that's the job you signed up for when you decided to let other people play with your creative children.

This is the collaborative chaos of filmmaking, where your script becomes everyone's script—and somehow, if you're lucky, skilled and diplomatic enough, it might still resemble something you're proud to have written.

CHAPTER 11

THE GOOD, THE BAD AND THE AWFUL

THREADING THROUGH THE HOLLYWOOD HILLS, I was running late to a meeting, each turn adding another layer of stress to my already fraying nerves. As anyone who's driven them knows, the roads in the hills are a sadistic puzzle designed by someone who clearly hated both cars and sanity. The anxiety before meetings used to grip me like a vise, but somewhere along the way, it loosened its hold. Maybe it was the small taste of success I'd had, or maybe the meetings had just become routine, so they'd lost their power to intimidate.

Being late wasn't my style. In this business, punctuality isn't just professional courtesy—it's survival. When you're asking someone to bet on you, the least you can do is respect their time. But there was another reason I was obsessive about being early: Back when I was just another broke screenwriter, I drove a car that looked like it had survived three apocalypses. The humiliation of having the worst vehicle in the studio lot was a special kind of torture. I'd park blocks away, with my vehicle out of sight, and fast-walk (sometimes run) through the LA heat, hoping to arrive looking presentable.

At the time, my pre-owned Audi let me pull right up front

without a second thought. But the Hills have their own way of keeping you humble. Just when the streets reach their most byzantine—where logic and urban planning seem to have taken a permanent vacation—that's when technology inevitably fails you. The GPS signal disappears, a universal experience for anyone who's ever navigated the Hollywood Hills. It's a reminder that no matter how far you've come, these streets can still make you feel like an interloper.

Perched in the Hills, Clive Barker's compound commanded attention—two adjacent mansions, each serving a distinct purpose. One was his residence, the other his creative sanctuary: a studio filled with his artwork and a bustling production office for his book and film projects. I stood before the entrance of the studio, faced with a door that seemed more suited to a medieval fortress than a Hollywood home. Its size alone was impressive, but its history would prove even more intriguing.

The scale of the property made sense for someone of Barker's stature. Since emerging in the 1980s, he'd fundamentally reshaped horror and dark fantasy, earning Stephen King's endorsement after his *Books of Blood* collection. The creator of *Hellraiser* had gone on to become one of the most influential voices in horror—selling millions of books and building an empire of nightmares that spanned literature, film and visual arts.

I was there because Clive Barker's development team had taken a liking to our horror script *Damned*, and they wanted to chat about some of their projects in the pipeline. A veteran of Barker's creative team named Rob opened the massive door—later explaining that it was an authentic piece salvaged from an English castle and transported across the Atlantic. The interior matched the gothic grandeur of its entrance.

Every hallway served as a gallery, showcasing Barker's unsettling paintings that had a Dante-meets-lurid-sex vibe.

We sat down with Rob and talked shop about what we were working on and what they had brewing. Then Rob leaned over the massive gothic desk and said, "We've got a project in the TV horror space, and we need someone to write the pilot." He smiled wide. "The executive producers are Clive and possibly Quentin Tarantino."

The names hit like a double shot of Jameson. *Tarantino and Barker? Did I hear that right?* Rob continued, "I think you guys would be perfect for this. I'm going to see what I can do—I want to work with you on this project." We floated out of that gloomy fever dream of a compound high on possibility. I called my agent, spreading the gospel of good news like a true believer. He made all the right noises and promised to push it forward. Why wouldn't he? I'd just done the genre director hat trick by working with Ferrara, Argento and Carpenter. Next up was Barker...I felt the stars were aligned.

The next day, I got a call from Rob. His voice had the kind of tone that makes your stomach drop before the words even hit. "Your agent screwed you," he said, flat and cold as morgue steel. "He pitched another writing team—guys with a bigger quote and more credits."

A "quote" in screenwriting refers to a writer's established minimum payment rate based on their most recent paid writing jobs. It's essentially the baseline price tag for their services, determined by their track record in the industry.

For example, if a writer has a quote of $300,000 per script, a production company with a low budget might not be able to afford them—even if they love the writer's work. Conversely, having a high quote can make a writer more attractive to major studios, as it implies a proven track record of success.

What our crafty agent didn't know was that Rob and I went to high school together. In the cutthroat world of deal-making, under normal circumstances we'd never have been told what happened. This was different. I'd known Rob since we were teenagers. We went to high school parties together, drank cheap beer and obsessed over bands like U2 and The Alarm. If I trust anyone in this business, it's someone I grew up with—not a fast-talking, deal-making agent.

The betrayal landed like a knife in the ribs—the guy who was supposed to be building our career was sabotaging it. That's a horror story all its own.

We did what any self-respecting writer would do: We fired the agent.

The TV show? Died on the vine like so many promising projects in this town. That other writing team the agent pitched? They're still out there, grinding away in the trenches. Not superstars, not failures—just survivors in the middle ground of the industry. They've had careers that are parallel to mine.

The ex-agent? He turned out to be a Hollywood king-maker. These days, he's swimming in success, with a track record of orchestrated spec script deals that would make Midas blush. He's transformed nobodies into somebodies, guided careers into the stratosphere and probably earned enough in commissions to buy a small country.

He's exactly what he always was—a shark who knows how to close a deal. When I needed him most, he was someone else's shark.

That agent fiasco turned out to be an anomaly in a career full of brilliant representation. But I've never forgotten what it felt like to get screwed over by someone who was supposed to be on my team. It crystallized something essential about this business: Nobody is coming to save you. Not your agent, not your manager or the producer who loves your script. In Hollywood, you're always your own first line of defense. The moment you forget that, the moment you assume someone else has your best interests at heart, you're already dead in the water.

CHAPTER 12

AMERICAN HORROR STORY
(OF DEVELOPMENT)

I WAS SPRAWLED on my couch, watching *Flavor of Love* reruns on MTV. My dog, Junior, sat next to me, giving me that look—you know the one—that mixture of pity and judgment. The absurdity of the situation hit me like a brick: Here I was, a supposedly functioning adult, watching D-list celebrities compete for the affections of a man wearing a giant clock around his neck. I called the cable company right then and there, cut the cord and took my dog for a long walk to clear the shame from my system.

With no TV distractions, I focused on film history. I mainlined French New Wave and Italian neorealism and binged on '70s revenge flicks like *Rolling Thunder*. I hunted down questionable masterpieces like Cimino's *Year of the Dragon* and watched the Kubrick classic *Barry Lyndon* multiple times. From *The Third Man* to *The Getaway*, I consumed it all with the desperate intensity of someone making up for lost time. Because let's face it—if you're going to call yourself a professional screenwriter, you'd better be well-versed in the actual medium you want to create.

Once I had begun to establish my career in features, I

started hearing in reverential tones that a new golden age of television had begun.

I decided to give TV a second chance. I put on the new version of *Battlestar Galactica* and had my mind completely rewired. This wasn't the mindless pablum I'd sworn off years ago. This was something else entirely—complex, ambitious and adult storytelling. The age of TiVo and streaming had killed off the predictable procedural cop shows that dominated the airwaves for decades. In their place were now long-form, challenging narratives. I crawled back to the cable company and surrendered to this brave new world of impending peak TV.

Around the time of my new admiration for TV, I found myself grappling with an expansive screenplay idea—one that felt too vast and unwieldy to be contained within a standard 110-page script. Frustrated but determined, I floated the idea to my writing partner. Without missing a beat, we decided to pivot and tackle a TV pilot instead.

I reached out to my manager, asking for a few pilot scripts to study their format—a task far more challenging then than it would be today, when nearly every TV show script is just a quick internet search away.

The project was titled *The 13*, an alternative history series imagining a world where the United States lost its war of independence over 200 years ago, leaving it under perpetual British control. In this envisioned America, citizens were relegated to third-class status: denied access to higher education, banned from flying on planes and forced into monotonous, industrial dead-end jobs—all as a lingering punishment for a rebellion that had taken place centuries before.

At its heart, the show followed a daring group of American insurgents—labeled as terrorists by the regime—as they sought to ignite a second revolution. The narrative was a tapestry of richly drawn characters, intricate political and personal intrigue and expansive world-building. For example, in this alternate reality, Native American tribes had allied with the British, securing vast oil reserves in the Midwest. The tribes cruised around in fleets of Range Rovers, their newfound wealth transforming them into influential oil barons with more money than they knew what to do with.

Over the next few months, we finished the pilot and pitch. With no TV agent in our corner, my ever-resourceful manager shot the pilot off to a slew of agencies. We eventually signed with a guy at Paradigm who was, quite simply, one of the best damn agents in the business—hardworking, passionate about our material, honest and blunt.

This guy wasted no time. He had us pitching our idea to over 20 production companies in a manic blitz, and several companies wanted to bite. Then the bidding war exploded. In the midst of our pitch frenzy, Lionsgate requested we meet for an 8 am breakfast to deliver their hard sell. If someone sets up a breakfast meeting with you, they really want the project. Within minutes, Lionsgate emerged as the undisputed winner. Their first order of business was to overhaul our pitch—eight to 10 minutes flat, no more. They insisted we keep our pitch razor-sharp and not mention that we even had a pilot. Their logic was to let the networks and streamers fall for the idea first, then tempt them with the script.

(For the uninitiated: Pitching a TV show is like playing musical chairs. First, you woo a production company—the folks with the track record and clout to lock in a deal with a streaming giant like Netflix. Then you and the production company hit the road, pitching to networks until you inch closer to that elusive green light.)

Lionsgate's plan? It fucking worked perfectly.

In one frenetic week, we found ourselves in 25-plus meetings with buyers. We were out there with the Lionsgate team and our producer Allison Shearmur—a film producer and ex-studio executive with a pedigree that included shepherding franchises like *The Bourne Identity* and *The Hunger Games*. Every meeting unfolded like a well-rehearsed routine: We'd deliver our eight-to-10-minute pitch, chat about the show and then the Lionsgate exec would lean in and ask, "What did you think of the pilot?" Each time, their response was identical: "You don't have a pilot?" The exec would then calmly pull out his phone and say, "I thought you had it—the assistant's sending it over right now."

Watching him pull this trick over and over was like witnessing a masterclass in Hollywood's sleight of hand—a clear demarcation between the pretenders and the road-tested pros.

We pitched to Netflix, HBO and Starz—basically anyone making TV. Then, in the oddest twist of fate, both ABC and NBC expressed interest. Two major networks clamoring for a show about terrorists? At that time, Netflix and the other streamers were still the new kids in town—networks reigned supreme.

One morning the TV agent called.

If you receive a call from your reps before lunchtime, you're kicking ass. It means you're at the front of the client line. You're closing deals, producers love your new script and studios and directors want to work with you. If you get the afternoon call, things are moving—the agent or manager still has faith in you and your ability to close deals and generate income. Maybe they have a possible open writing assignment you might be good for or want to team you up with a producer who likes your sample. If you get the call after 6 (which is usually the case if you're a working writer and not an A-list ass-kicker), it means they're politely doing a quick check-in. They've got nothing for you; they're propping you up so you stay enthusiastic about your career and send over a new TV idea or spec—anything they can work with.

That morning, our TV agent called at 8:30 to say that ABC wanted the show and were going straight to 13 episodes. Before the advent of Netflix and streamers, this was the equivalent of hitting a home run. Basically, it meant a network wanted your show so much, they would guarantee to make the first 13 episodes if you made a deal with them.

I quickly did the math in my head. If they made 13 episodes—I'd make a million fucking dollars.

"I'm a goddamn millionaire!" I yelled.

My dog jumped back, slightly fearful for a beat. I'm not one to show a lot of emotion (outside of telling someone to fuck off), so he was unaccustomed to joyous outbursts.

Our agent called back three hours later.

"They want the show, but they're not going to commit to 13 right out the gate," he explained.

He had jumped the gun. Felt good to be an imaginary millionaire, if only for a few hours.

After another round of bidding chaos, we signed a deal with ABC. I was a little surprised that a network that made *Grey's Anatomy* wanted a hard, cutting-edge show where the good guys were basically terrorists engaged in kidnapping, sabotage and assassinations. I figured Max or Showtime might be into something like this—but a network?

Our first creative meeting at ABC happened not long after. They loved the pilot and had paid us a ton of money, so I was looking forward to it. On arrival there was a conference room filled with executives waiting to talk about the show and how they envisioned it.

They all had notes.

The same pitch and pilot that had everyone drooling and calling our work sheer brilliance suddenly became a Rorschach test for each executive's opinion. Notes came in by the dozen: ABC had notes, Lionsgate had notes on those notes, our producer had notes on top of that and even the president of ABC tossed in his two cents. It was filmmaking by committee—a minefield where you smile through the chaos, nod politely and internally curse the absurdity of it all.

If I were Scorsese or Tarantino, I could say, "Fuck off, it's great; leave it be." But I'm not. You either play ball or get out of the game.

In one particularly memorable creative meeting, we sat at a table surrounded by a gaggle of execs—at least 12 of them—each armed with ideas. You learn quickly: Take every suggestion with grace, push back just enough to avoid looking like a pushover, and remember that these buyers are now your overlords paying you to rewrite your own pilot. At one point, we received a 15-page document of combined notes on our 60-page pilot. The kicker? Some pages demanded we cut all the flashbacks while others insisted on expanding them to reveal every last secret. What the fuck were we supposed to do?

Then the bombshell: They decided to bring in a top-tier showrunner—a guy who already had a hit show or two under his belt and, in the golden era of TV, was considered godlike.

I was excited at the thought of collaborating with this huge showrunner, ready to unleash every ounce of my creative genius. I figured any day he'd call to discuss the project and get our take, then we'd get to work on our show.

Days went by. Then weeks.

He never called.

He never emailed.

He never met with us.

He treated us like the hooker who had already been paid and should just pack up and go home.

He never exchanged a single word with our producer

either. Instead, he unilaterally decided to rewrite the pilot from scratch, completely sidelining the writers who'd birthed the show and sold it to both Lionsgate and ABC.

Worse yet, I was informed by our attorney that with him rewriting the pilot, under WGA rules he could strip my partner and me of any writing credit—reducing us to mere executive producers with zero creative say.

One executive bluntly told me, "This happens more often than you'd think. You do all the work, and then a hotshot showrunner swoops in and takes control. If you're not established, you're toast."

We never even got to see the new pilot the showrunner turned in. Maybe it was all part of some complicated, devious game he knew how to play. If he never talked to us, he could pretend that all the ideas in the new pilot were his. He had 25-plus years in the TV business; we'd been in it for months. He knew the angles inside and out. When you don't know how the business works, it's easy to get screwed.

The pilot he created was promptly killed by ABC. Just like that, our TV dream died. To this day, I still haven't heard from the showrunner.

Years later, someone at ABC slipped me a copy of his version of the pilot. I'll say it—the thing was a piece of shit.

This unmade show remains the biggest regret of my career. It could have been transformative TV—at a time when the medium was exploding—and I was damn proud of its creative vision and how, as a team, we'd navigated our way to ABC's doorstep. Not only was it a creative, intriguing show, it also would have been a financial jackpot.

To this day, TV execs ask me how this amazing pilot didn't get made. I try to put the showrunner out of my head and say something like, "That's the business."

CHAPTER 13
THE GREAT TV SHOW ROBBERY

THE PHONE CALL came like a guillotine. The attorney's voice cut through the line:

"You're facing a pending lawsuit."

"Lawsuit? For what?" was my confused response.

"Stealing someone's idea," he replied. His words hung in the air like a bad smell.

I was still basking in the euphoria of my first big break in TV. Filled with optimism, we had just sold our pilot *The 13* to ABC. This was before the avalanche of notes, and long before the showrunner hijacked the project.

There were articles and announcements in all the Hollywood trades. The story even trended on Reddit. It was a moment that should have been my coronation into the kingdom of television. Before I could pop the top on a cheap bottle of champagne to celebrate, I found myself caught in the crosshairs of a possible intellectual property lawsuit.

The accusers were a group of nobodies—three writers and a producer I'd never heard of. Only the producer had any IMDb credits, and they were all on micro-budget films. I had never met any of these people, yet they were claiming I'd stolen their idea.

The kicker? They had somehow engaged a huge and powerful firm to take on their case. Lionsgate seemed slightly impressed that they had hired a legit law firm—one with over 1,000 attorneys and an 86 percent litigation win rate. These weren't ambulance chasers. They were stone-cold courtroom killers.

Their letter referenced the press the project had received and concluded that we had stolen their idea. Both projects had the same title, *The 13*. Both centered on an alternate world where the United States had lost the War of Independence in 1776 and had been under British control for over 200 years.

Look, I'll freely admit that the concept has been done before. Alternate history has been around forever. Take *The Man in the High Castle* by Philip K. Dick, for example. Dick's book imagines a world in which the Axis powers won World War II. The story occurs 15 years after the end of the war and depicts various characters living under the rule of Imperial Japan or Nazi Germany in a partitioned United States. That novel was one of the inspirations we used when writing the pilot (we sold our show two years before *The Man in the High Castle* became a TV show of its own). It was world-building centered on a big "what if."

I told the attorney the claim was total bullshit. He agreed but reminded me, "They've hired a really big law firm to come after you, so we need to take this seriously."

"Can they do this?" I asked.

He coolly responded, "They can try." He then asked me a series of questions to understand the situation.

The questions went on and on, and every answer was "no." He stated he'd investigate the situation and advised us to document every step of the project—every draft, every file that ever existed.

There's nothing worse than being made to feel like an idea

thief when the concept and the subsequent work you created were all yours. Our journey to this moment wasn't some overnight success. It was a two-year marathon of writing.

A day or two later, the Lionsgate attorney emailed me a copy of the letter.

The letter stated, "Their clients are being denied credit and compensation by virtue of the theft of their idea and treatment, and are amenable to a possible amicable resolution."

My response? "Fuck these guys."

Lionsgate spoke with their attorney, and he relayed to me that they weren't messing around. They were demanding half the rights to the show, half the money we'd made, half of any future earnings and credit for creating the show. If we didn't comply, they'd take us to court and force us to defend ourselves —a costly proposition.

Again, I thought, *Fuck these guys*.

What we found was that this producer and two writers had submitted a treatment to CAA (the largest Agency in Hollywood). I didn't know what was in their treatment. I do know that what made *The 13* great was the high-concept world we'd built, centered on a group of characters with deep backstories and relationships fraught with tension and drama.

The Lionsgate attorney laid out his plan: Don't respond until every piece of information is compiled, then hit them all at once.

As we assembled our case over the next two weeks, the high-powered attorney representing the accusers sent increasingly aggressive and insulting emails.

We discovered that the group accusing us of theft had created only a pitch—and registered it with the WGA and sent it to CAA? Confusing. Meanwhile, we had a pitch, a full pilot and had filed for copyright a year before selling the show.

But here's the fascinating part of this industry: How do two completely separate teams conjure nearly identical concepts?

It's not magic but the well-worn paths of commercial storytelling.

I know a producer who believes that once you think of an idea, it exists somewhere in the ether—and someone else can latch onto it subconsciously. Personally, I think the reason is that when you're coming up with a film or TV project, the ideas usually have a commercial hook. Imagine a box—a very small, very restrictive box. That's studio storytelling, on both the film and TV sides. Three-act structure. Character arcs. Redemption. The second-act turn. When these formulas get beaten into your head repeatedly, creativity starts to look suspiciously similar across different projects.

For example, I had an idea for a feature 10 years ago about a secret FBI facility that had been capturing and studying serial killers for decades. When a tornado tears through the town where the killers are housed in an underground facility, they all escape. After years of confinement and testing, it's on. The citizens of the town are now caught in the crosshairs of these deranged murderers. Since the tornado knocked out all communications, a lone sheriff's deputy has to protect the town until help arrives. The killers were all riffs on classic cinematic villains like Michael Myers and Jason. It was bloody, gory and fun. After 10 years of pitching the idea in meetings, I decided to finally write the script.

Then I saw a trailer for a new NBC show called *The Hunting Party*. Here's the synopsis:

"*The Hunting Party* begins with a catastrophic explosion. While disasters that cause major loss of life and destruction are always horrific, this blast has even more profound ramifications. The Pit, a highly classified prison and home to the most violent and dangerous criminals on Earth, has been leveled. Even worse, not all the prisoners are accounted for. Desperate to keep their dirty secret under wraps while rounding up the escaped sociopaths, the government enlists former FBI profiler Bex Henderson, who begins building a task force to hunt them down one by one."

In another strangely similar scenario, Netflix released *Day Shift* in 2022. The trailer and synopsis were almost identical to our sample script *LA Gothic*, which had been read by countless executives and producers over the last 15 years.

As an ice breaker from time to time, I'd open general meetings with what I thought was my ace in the hole—my personal contribution to Hollywood's recycling of bad ideas. The pitch went like this: A gang of adrenaline-junkie bikers chase tornadoes across the Midwest, using the chaos as cover to rob banks while the locals cower in storm cellars. One of them dies in the opening heist (because of course he does), and in comes our hero—an ex-motorcycle racing champion turned FBI agent, who goes deep undercover to take them down. It's *Point Break* with motorcycles and tornadoes.

I'd pitch it as a joke. Until someone sold a spec script with nearly the exact same idea—and for a lot of money.

This isn't an anomaly. It's just another Tuesday in the film and TV business.

I've been in countless meetings where I pitch an idea and the executive across the table says, "We've got something just like that."

You know what I'm *not* going to do about those projects that are eerily similar to my ideas? I'm not going to hire a high-powered attorney to go after the creators. I'm a professional. I move on and come up with 10 or 20 more pitches. I didn't pin my career on one idea.

What our accusers didn't know was the depth of our project's history. We'd been developing *The 13* for years—first as a feature film, then evolving it into a TV pilot when the concept became too expansive for a two-hour runtime. We had emails. We had drafts. We had a paper trail over three years old that would make a bureaucrat weep.

Their entire claim hinged on a treatment submitted to CAA—but they couldn't even specify who had received it. An assistant? Someone in the mailroom? This was their legal strategy to obtain half our show?

Here's the kicker: A year before their submission, CAA's TV department had already read our pilot. We'd even met with them about representation.

When the Lionsgate attorney lined up our project's time-line—beat by beat, date by date—it was like watching a legal symphony. He didn't just defend us. He wrote a magnum opus of a letter, obliterating their claims.

Less than 24 hours after his email, their attorney sent a reply—a sheepish surrender stating:

"Having seen that your clients' development of *The 13* evidently began before my clients' work on that theme, and that there are dissimilarities between the two approaches, my clients have concluded that the similarities and timing result from one of life's coincidences and not any improper activity. My clients will not bring any claim and wish your clients well with their project. Thank you for your courtesy in allaying my clients' concerns."

Fuck. These. Guys.

I called the Lionsgate attorney to thank him for believing our side of the story and burying these jokers.

He coldly replied, "I always knew they were full of shit. Their attorney knew they were full of shit. This happens all the time when dealing with a high-profile project that gets a lot of press—it was a shakedown."

I learned a valuable lesson from that experience: Everyone is trying to make it in this business. Some get by on talent, while others are just trying to seize an opportunity from your hard work.

CHAPTER 14

GAME OF DEATH (AND RESURRECTION)

EARLY IN MY SCREENWRITING CAREER, I was nursing a coffee at a café in LA when a familiar face appeared. It was a producer I knew, and he needed a script—fast. He had the financing lined up, provided the project met specific parameters.

"What parameters?" I asked, sipping my coffee.

"One location," he replied. "We don't want to move the crew or change wardrobe. It's gotta be an action film. Not too many speaking parts—we've got around $500,000 to make it."

I nodded, intrigued. "What about characters?"

"The lead has to be badass. Lots of fighting. We've got this famous MMA fighter in mind. He can't act, doesn't speak English well, so keep his lines to a minimum."

I waited for more details. "What about storyline?"

"You're smart. You'll figure it out."

It was a paid gig—a whopping $2,500 to write the script. If the film got made, I'd get another $15,000. My deal was $1,250 up front, the rest on completion. Enough to cover a month's rent, buy groceries and pay for a steady stream of Coors Light at the bar down the street. Back then, I was just starting out. I'd optioned a few scripts for peanuts, but this was my first "real" paycheck. I wasn't in the WGA, so I took the deal.

I had a month to deliver the script and burned through the up-front money without writing a word. When I realized the deadline was Monday, it was already Friday afternoon. Panic set in.

I thought about great action films set in a single location. *Die Hard?* Too iconic. *Assault on Precinct 13?* Too edgy. Then it hit me: Bruce Lee's *Game of Death.* At one point, Lee fights his way up a pagoda, each level presenting a tougher opponent.

That's it.

I'd do something like *Game of Death,* but in a different setting.

I chose a hospital. Our hero would fight his way up, floor by floor, to reach his goal. I'd make him a bodyguard, and at the top floor would be his boss, shot and wounded in the first scene of the film. He'd have to fight his way up to protect the boss. Each floor's adversaries? Assassins sent to finish the job. The twist? The hero isn't a bodyguard—he's actually the assassin, and the killers are the bodyguards. A semi-smart spin on a dumb shoot-'em-up.

I hammered out the script in a weekend.

A few months later, the producer called: They had sent the script to Wesley Snipes and he wanted to do it. With Snipes attached, it had suddenly become a film with a $10 million budget.

I'd foolishly mentioned it was inspired by *Game of Death,* so the producers unimaginatively named it exactly that. I fought that decision—I felt it disrespected Bruce Lee's legacy—but lost. There was some loophole that let them use the title.

I was originally told it would be a half-million-dollar film, so I'd put in my contract that I'd be paid $15,000 if it got made. That's fair for a $500K film—but not a $10 million one starring

Snipes. The producer's attorney quickly sent me a $15K check, hoping I'd cash it and lock myself into the deal.

If I had, I'd have been stuck.

On a $10 million film, the screenplay was worth two percent of the budget. I should've been paid around $200,000.

Luckily, I understood a little about how films work—and the importance of a clean chain of title, the contracts governing the rights of the film.

I made a video of myself ripping up the $15K check and sent it to them. I told them they couldn't make the film unless they paid me fairly. By not accepting the check, I hadn't been paid for the film. It was mostly a bluff, but the threat scared them.

One of the producers—who loved to brag about how powerful he was in the film business, yet stayed at a motel in Sherman Oaks and wore the same ill-fitting Ed Hardy shirt every time I saw him—called me.

"If you don't take the $15K, you'll never work in this business again."

My response: "Fuck off." Then I hung up.

A few days later, that same producer sheepishly called back to renegotiate my deal.

They left for Detroit to make the film with Snipes, Ernie Hudson, Zoe Bell and Robert Davi. I stayed in LA, satisfied with my renegotiated deal. Then I got another call.

"We need you in Detroit for a few days to work on the script."

"Why?"

"We hired a director. Abel Ferrara. He wants changes."

Hearing Ferrara's name changed everything.

Abel Ferrara is one of my cinematic idols—the filmmaker behind *King of New York*, *Bad Lieutenant*, and *Ms. 45*. His films are gritty, provocative and raw. I caught the next flight to Detroit.

When I met Abel, we went straight to the hotel bar (this was before he got sober). His reputation as a chaotic, maniacal director? Not true. He was funny, sharp and opinionated—a New Yorker with a story about everything. We talked about football, filmmaking, Little Italy and women. He was everything I hoped he'd be.

He liked the script but had changes in mind. Together, we worked on a new version during pre-production. He even invited me to auditions—rare for a writer. There wasn't much of an audition process. Abel didn't care about reading scenes. He talked to actors about their lives, who they were as people. He was casting humans, not performances. When I later directed my own film, I copied his approach.

We worked on the script every night at the hotel bar.

The surrounding area looked like a war zone. The doormen warned me not to walk more than three blocks from the hotel— I could get robbed or shot.

Inside the hotel, the bar became a nightly party. Crews from other films—the *Red Dawn* remake, *You Don't Know Jack* starring Al Pacino—were staying there, too.

The producers knew about the new script Abel and I had written, but they hadn't told Snipes because they feared he'd quit if he didn't like the changes. A few days before principal photography began, two scripts were floating around the production office. Hours before the first day of filming, they finally decided on one and picked ours.

I thought that was that: smooth sailing ahead as we started the shoot.

I was wrong.

Production started 10 hours late. Snipes didn't like his suit

—or something. Abel and I spent the day drinking beers in a hidden storage closet, swapping stories.

When filming finally started, it went downhill fast.

A few days in, Snipes stopped talking to Abel. Then he stopped talking to me after I questioned one of his ideas that didn't make sense. A film where the star won't speak to the director or writer? It was doomed.

The film spiraled.

After two weeks, a new set of producers arrived. I thought the original producers were going to end up in a trunk somewhere.

Instead, Abel and I were fired.

The new producers butchered the script. Scenes were added and removed by committee. One producer's girlfriend even ended up credited as a co-writer.

In the new version, the film opened with Snipes talking in a church. Then talking on a park bench. Then talking in a van. Ten solid minutes of dialogue to open a Wesley Snipes action movie. My version opened with a fight in an ambulance.

In the end, I got paid around $150,000. I worked with one of my idols, spent almost three months in Detroit and learned a valuable lesson: If you're working on a piece of shit, at least get paid.

Sony released the film. The producer who said I'd never work again? He disappeared.

Years later, the whole mess came back.

In 2017, one of the producers from *Game of Death*—and the same Sony executive—was making a film called *Kill 'Em All* with Jean-Claude Van Damme. Out of curiosity, I asked them what the film was about. They were cagey. They mumbled something about an action film.

Then I saw the trailer.

My heart sank. I recognized the story. It was my script.

Kill 'Em All was a recycled version of my original *Game of Death* script. They'd changed character names and added some lame backstory, but 98 percent of it was mine.

They thought I wouldn't notice. Or find out.

I called my attorney. Through a network of filmmaker friends, I was able to track down a copy of the shooting script—and confirmed the worst. It was my old script: The only real changes were the character names.

I called the producers and unleashed hell.

They argued they had the right to do it since they'd bought the original script. Legally, they straddled the line. Ethically, they crossed it.

They quickly proposed a settlement. They'd pay me some money now, cover my legal fees and if there was a sequel, they promised I'd be paid even more.

Years later, I wrote *Kill 'Em All 2*. Why not? I would be paid twice off the same script, once for writing and the other for the settlement fee—or so I thought.

Sony released *Kill 'Em All 2* in December 2024 and it hit the top 10 on Netflix, reaching No. 4 over the Christmas holidays.

While I was paid for the script on *Kill 'Em All 2*, I'm still waiting to be paid for that first *Kill 'Em All* settlement.

CHAPTER 15

TOTAL WRONG RECALL

ONE MORNING, I drove onto the Universal Studios lot filled with excitement. We had a meeting set up to discuss a sci-fi script called *Intelligence*.

Universal had a mandate to make mid-budget sci-fi films, and our script fit the bill. It was about a team of government scientists reverse-engineering a crashed UFO, only to discover —at the film's second-act turn—that the military hangar they were working in was actually an elaborate set inside a massive alien spaceship, much like *The Truman Show*. The aliens had tricked the team into revealing how Earth would defend itself in an invasion. It had *Twilight Zone* smarts with a third-act adrenaline rush of *Aliens* meets *The Great Escape*. A Universal executive we knew—a sci-fi junkie—had set up a meeting with a studio heavyweight. Let's call him Mr. Greenlight—one of those rare executives who could green-light a film in the room. If this meeting went well, we could walk out of Universal with a studio deal.

I pulled up to the security gate, bracing for the usual nonsense. Studio drive-ons are a gauntlet of miscommunication: wrong gates, misspelled names and forgotten appointments. When wires get crossed, security makes you sit there like an asshole while they try to verify your meeting. Nothing worse than getting your car pulled to the side as studio regulars cruise by in Range Rovers while you sit there looking like an interloping schmuck.

Parking at a studio lot is its own adventure. Every studio has limited parking, and you're told exactly where to park. Finding that elusive spot can make Indiana Jones' search for the Holy Grail look easy. Once you're parked, you're left to navigate the lot itself—and most studios have been around for decades, expanding and remodeling over time. It's not unusual to find Building 72 next to Bungalow 632, across from the Old Executive Building.

But that day, luck was on my side. I sailed through the guard gate without a hitch and found parking easily. I took it as a good omen: Everything was working according to plan.

While waiting for Mr. Greenlight to arrive, we went over our pitch one last time. Strategy was locked: highlight successful sci-fi films, project confidence and emphasize why the studio should make *Intelligence*. This was a sure thing.

Mr. Greenlight entered the bungalow with an air of authority. He was cold, emotionless. *Fine*. I could handle that. *Just stick to the pitch and sell the project.*

He took his seat and immediately started talking. He was in a hurry, which I mistook for enthusiasm. He told us the script was great—intelligent sci-fi didn't land on his desk very often. He loved the tone. He was impressed with the writing.

We were in.

In my head, I was already daydreaming. How much would we get paid? Who would star? Who would direct? A Universal film...I couldn't wait to humble-brag to all my writer friends.

Mr. Greenlight kept going: He loved the structure, the vivid characters.

I had to hide my excitement. No one likes a giddy writer, especially not studio execs.

Then he said, "I love that part of the story when they reach the meteor."

Wait. Did he just say meteor? There's no meteor in our script.

Maybe he misspoke.

Then he went into detail about the mission on the meteor, how he loved the depth of the characters revealed in the flashbacks.

We didn't have any flashbacks.

That's when the full extent of the disaster hit me.

He wasn't talking about our script.

Somehow, Mr. Greenlight had read the wrong project. Either he was given the wrong script or the wrong coverage. Whatever the reason, this was bad.

And here's the thing: You never want to tell the person who can green-light your project that they're wrong about anything. You massage the situation. You never give them a reason to dislike you—or your project.

But this was different.

I looked over at the exec who'd championed the project. We exchanged a look: *What now?* We sat in silence as Mr. Greenlight kept talking, blissfully unaware.

Finally, the exec couldn't take it anymore.

"You might have read the wrong script."

Those seven words killed the meeting.

Mr. Greenlight froze, stared at us with pure contempt and said his assistant must've given him the wrong script. He gathered his notes and stormed out.

I knew then: This project was dead.

I was right. We never heard from Mr. Greenlight again.

I don't know if he ever even read our script.

Over time, I've learned the hard way: Never make an executive feel dumb. Early in my career, I thought the way to impress studio execs was to be the smartest guy in the room. I'd rattle off obscure film references: *The Long Good Friday, Mona Lisa, Manhunter, To Live and Die in L.A.* or *Tenebrae.* I'd bring up characters like Harry Lime and Lord Bullingdon. I thought I'd be rewarded for showcasing my encyclopedic film knowledge.

Wrong.

What I didn't realize was that the last thing you want to do is reference a film an executive hasn't seen. It makes them feel excluded. It makes them feel dumb.

And no one in this business likes to feel dumb.

That wasn't the last time wires got crossed on a project.

One of my first feature ideas was a zombie plague concept where the infection only affected people once they stopped growing. It left a world of kids forced to band together to survive. I pitched it as *Night of the Living Dead* meets *The Breakfast Club*, with heavy *Omega Man* influence.

I ran into a producer I knew at a coffee shop and casually pitched the idea. She loved it. She said she had a young director who'd be perfect for it.

A week later, my agent called: A high-profile production company wanted to pay me to write the script.

Easy money.

Then came the call with the production company. They loved the castle setting. They loved that the story took place decades after the zombie outbreak.

Wait—what? My version was set in San Diego, a few weeks after the outbreak. Kids raiding malls, fending off juvenile detention escapees with a *Lord of the Flies* vibe and a touch of *Return of the Living Dead.*

This was different.

Turns out, the director had pitched his own spin on the idea to the production company. While the core conceit was the same, the setting and tone were completely different. His version was *Reign of Fire* with zombies.

Then I was told the production company wanted to meet in person to discuss the script. My writing partner at the time was out of town, so I went in solo.

I thought we were meeting to talk about ideas.

I was ushered into a conference room with 10 executives from two companies, the director and his manager, who represented some of the biggest writer-directors in the business. They expected me to pitch the full outline on the spot.

I had nothing.

I wasn't about to point at the director and say, "Ask him—it's his version." Throwing someone under the bus in front of a room like that? Instant career suicide.

So, I sat there, staring at this firing squad of seasoned producers. I hadn't prepared to give a full take on a bastardized version of my idea. I'm good at winging it in the room, but at that moment I had nothing.

Finally I said, "I'll tell you the outline when you pay me."

Silence.

As soon as the words left my mouth, I knew: *wrong answer.*

I tried to recover but the damage was done.

Ten minutes after leaving that meeting, my phone blew up. My agent, my manager and the producers—they all wanted to know what the hell happened. I did damage control, apologized to everyone and tried to salvage the project.

Eventually, we worked out an outline based on the director's version. We were paid to write the script, but it never had the energy or urgency of the original concept. It wasn't anyone's fault. Everyone involved loved the idea; they just had different visions for it.

At that stage in my career, I didn't know how to juggle competing visions and merge them into something coherent.

I was still under the illusion that I was an "artist," and that my writing talent alone would carry me. What I didn't understand yet was that having writing skills is only half the job. The other half is diplomacy—understanding that everyone in the room has a stake in the project. Everyone wants to make a good film. Everyone's job is on the line.

The script was fun. It had cool characters. It took place in a run-down castle in the future, with teenagers fighting zombies.

And like most projects in the film business...it never had a chance.

CHAPTER 16

INDECENT FINANCIAL PROPOSALS

ONE DAY, I opened my email to read over my executive producer agreement for a film I'd co-written. Under "Payment," it said: $1.00.

Yes. One dollar.

This was the first time I was receiving an Executive Producer credit on a film where I was also the writer. It had to be a typo. The budget of the film was over $10 million.

I called my attorney in a panic. As I speed-talked through the WTF of my contract, he interrupted in a calm voice, "I did this so you wouldn't get fucked."

I took a deep breath, stopped talking and let him explain.

"If I set up your deal where all your money is paid for the screenplay, it's tied to the rights. Producers can't screw with your pay once that's agreed to. If they did, they'd mess up their rights to the script and their chain of title. They won't do it."

Okay, that I understood.

He moved on to the executive producer deal. "They can fire you as an executive producer and not pay your full salary. If they go over budget, the first thing they'll do is hold your salary. They can't fuck you if your money is tied to the script purchase."

My attorney—an ex-studio attorney—is good. He knows all the angles and has seen everything. I still structure all my deals like that to this day. And you know what happened, as it does on many independently financed films? Some of the producers didn't get their entire salaries.

I did. Thanks to my brilliant attorney.

Getting paid in film and TV is always an adventure. I've been hired to write scripts and pilots where closing the deal to get paid ends up taking longer than it did to write the script.

Here's what happens when you're hired. Your agent or attorney negotiates the deal: pay, credit, reversion of rights and other major points. That draft gets sent over to the business affairs department for the company that's hiring you, where an attorney drafts a deal. And unless you're a priority, that process can sometimes take weeks, even months.

You've been hired to write, but now you're sitting around waiting to start. You don't start until you get paid. You can't get paid until your deal is done. It's completely frustrating, especially if you need to pay the bills.

This has been such a problem in recent years that the WGA's latest agreement addressed the fact that most deals for writers move at a glacial pace.

In most deals, you get paid in three installments, kind of like a three-act structure. One to start, and you write out a treatment or outline of the work you're going to do. You send that to the studio. They give you notes on it. Then they send you off to write the script based on the approved outline/treatment. After you've turned in the script, they give you more notes, you implement them and when you deliver the screenplay, you get your last payment.

They can then hire you to do more rewrites if both parties agree. Or they can take your script and hire someone else to rewrite it without even telling you.

They paid for it. They own it. Once you turn in your script, you may never hear from that executive or studio again. It happens all the time. Best course of action: Move on to the next gig, job or spec.

Amnesia is your friend in this business. The faster you forget about the last project and don't look back, the better. Like a shark, you've got to keep moving to bring money in.

If you have an agent, once you turn in a project the agency has to send over an invoice. The agency then receives the check on your behalf, cashes it, takes out their 10 percent and reissues you a check.

Unbelievably, one time I had turned in a screenplay and needed the agency to send over an invoice so I could get the last payment. I emailed the agent and their assistant, asking if they could do this.

It never happened.

I asked again. And again.

Finally, after two weeks of cajoling, they sent over the invoice and I got my payment. The incredibly annoying thing? This job—which was with a major production company—wasn't even set up by the agent. So basically, the agency made $10,000 for sending three invoices.

And they couldn't even be bothered to do that.

CHAPTER 17

LAYER CAKE (OF PROBLEMS)

I'D REACHED that inevitable crossroads in my career where I realized I needed to stop writing exclusively about things that go bump in the night. Writing horror scripts is a great way to break into the film business, but I realized I was going to get classified as strictly a horror writer—and I had other cinematic interests. So it was time to pivot into thrillers, a genre that might actually open new doors instead of just revealing what was lurking behind them.

The question was: What kind of thriller would work as a proper calling card?

Then it hit me, like a brick through a London pub window: Write something like *The Long Good Friday*.

If you haven't seen *The Long Good Friday*, it's a masterpiece of British gangster cinema. Bob Hoskins plays Harold Shand, a London crime boss dreaming of legitimizing his empire through a massive docklands redevelopment project. Naturally, everything goes spectacularly wrong. His empire gets attacked. His associates start dying. In true British fashion, Harold responds by torturing every gangster in London until someone confesses to something.

The genius of the film lies in watching a street-smart operator completely lose his composure as his carefully constructed world crumbles around him. Desperation makes idiots of us all.

I've learned if you start with a film you genuinely love—and think, *What's my version of this type of film?*—you'll end up with something inspired by it, but ultimately different. Like covering a song: You honor the original, but it becomes your own.

My homage to *The Long Good Friday* became *Tokarev*—the story of Paul, a reformed criminal who's built a legitimate life: beautiful wife, teenage daughter and suburban bliss. He's buried his violent past until one night, while he and his wife are at a charity event, masked intruders break into their home, beat up his daughter's friends, kidnap her...and kill her.

Paul does what any grieving father with a particular set of skills would do: He calls up his old crew and wages a brutal campaign of revenge. The police tell him his daughter was killed with a Russian Tokarev pistol. Years earlier, Paul and his crew had robbed a Russian mobster—killing him with, of course, a Tokarev.

Paul assumes the Russians have come for payback. The violence escalates. Bodies drop. And then comes the twist: The Russians had nothing to do with it.

Paul's daughter wasn't murdered by gangsters. She died in a tragic accident. She and her friends had found Paul's old gun collection—including the Tokarev. One of her friends accidentally shot her. Panicked, the boys staged the kidnapping to cover their tracks.

The most devastating revelation? Paul's entire campaign of vengeance—everything he did—was for nothing. He'd reverted to being the monster he'd tried so hard to leave behind. And in doing so, he'd antagonized the Russians for no reason. They send their own killers after him, and Paul meets his end knowing it was all his fault.

Not exactly *The Long Good Friday*, but maybe its spiritual cousin—with more daddy issues.

I handed the script to my manager and agent. They loved it. Like, really loved it. They sent it out wide, and suddenly my calendar filled up with meetings. This script—this thriller—was opening doors that had stayed bolted shut during my horror phase.

Everyone said the same thing: They'd read hundreds of scripts and always figured out who the killer was by page 30. But *Tokarev* actually surprised them. They had suspects. They had theories. But the reveal blindsided them.

For the first time, I felt like I wasn't tricking my way into meetings. I'd written something solid. Something that impressed people across the board.

After a meeting at Warner Bros., one executive leaned forward and said, "I know who would love this...Antoine Fuqua. Can I send it to him?"

Fuck *yes*, you can send it to Antoine Fuqua.

This was the guy who directed *Training Day*. A filmmaker who understood both character and violence. He was perfect for the material—if he liked it.

I waited nervously for days.

Then the call came: Antoine wanted to meet.

Another *fuck yes*.

Fuqua is legitimately the coolest person on the planet. Smart. Calm. Charismatic. He knows film like a sommelier knows wine. I liked him instantly and wanted nothing more than for him to direct this script. He optioned it quickly, planning for it to be his next film. He sent it to actors, who all responded.

Then, as happens in Hollywood, he got hired to direct one massive film...then another...and another. Our project got sidelined.

But before stepping away, Fuqua gave us a parting gift: He passed the script to Nicolas Cage.

Cage loved it. He and Fuqua had discussed doing it together. Cage agreed to stay attached if we found a director he approved of.

In Hollywood, that's like finding a unicorn that does your taxes.

We brought on a young Spanish director whose first film showed promise. Cage approved. Danny Glover signed on. Suddenly, we were headed to Mobile, Alabama, to shoot what I still believed was an amazing script.

Here's where things started to go sideways.

In filmmaking, as the writer, you might get to pick one or two hills to die on. But once your script becomes a movie, it's the director's vision. And that's the end of it.

Tokarev opened with a flashback when our main characters are in their 20s, mid-heist, then jumps to the present day, when they're in their 40s. But in pre-production, we struggled to find actors who looked like younger versions of Cage and the others.

I suggested a solution: Have the younger versions wear masks during the opening heist, then use a tattoo or scar to reveal who's who later.

The director waved me off. "We don't need masks."

In the edit? The opening didn't work. The younger actors looked nothing like their older counterparts. The sequence was cut entirely.

So much for the heist where they sawed off a guy's hand chained to a briefcase full of diamonds. That would've been one hell of an opening.

Gone.

Then came casting. My girlfriend at the time, a talent manager, suggested a young, up-and-coming actress for Cage's daughter. The director dismissed her immediately: "She can't act."

She wasn't even given an audition.

Her name? Ana de Armas.

Another tragedy involved the female lead. In my script, she was Lady Macbeth—a ruthless operator in a world of criminals. In the film? She cried through every scene. Lines that were meant to be cold and calculating became soft and whimpering. The strongest character in the story was reduced to weakness.

To Cage's credit, he was a professional. He cared. He and I spent an hour discussing *Thief*—specifically the scene where James Caan and Tuesday Weld talk about their future in a diner. Cage suggested adding something like that to our film.

I pitched the idea. The producers agreed.

Then came the twist: I had 30 minutes to write the scene.

We were shooting in a restaurant, and Cage and Danny Glover were waiting. Eighty crew members. Two actors. All waiting on me.

This is when you find out whether you're really a screenwriter or just pretending.

I sat in a booth and wrote the scene. Glover's character tells Cage how years earlier, his son had been hit by a car. He wanted revenge but held back. It was an accident. He let the anger go.

Cage's character responds coldly, "But your kid's still alive."

Then he walks away.

I wrote it. They shot it. It worked.

But that wasn't the end of the drama. During post-production, more battles were fought. The US distributor decided to retitle the film *Rage*.

Not *Tokarev*.

Rage.

Cue the "Rage Cage" jokes. Thanks, marketing team.

The film debuted on Netflix. Financially, it did well. But creatively?

The film felt disjointed. What had been a tight, character-driven thriller was now just another direct-to-video revenge film. After four years of work, I wasn't in a better place as a screenwriter. I'd gotten paid. I'd made a film. But my career hadn't moved forward.

There was a screening at CAA. As the lights came up, my agent looked over and said, "At least you wrote a good script."

CHAPTER 18

A FEW GOOD WGA MEMBERS

I WAS USHERED into a surprisingly small room, following dozens of writers with stars in their eyes. I grabbed a seat in the back. Several men took the stage, perched above us like wizards looking over a group of eager acolytes ready to learn magic from the wisest and most powerful in their community.

We'd been shuffled into a small auditorium at the back of the Musicians' Credit Union—or something like that. All I know is this wasn't taking place in the WGA's massive eyesore of a building that sits on the corner of Third and Fairfax. The place had the look and feel of a larger version of the basement from *Goodfellas*, the one where Tommy gets whacked. I thought for a beat: *I hope that getting-whacked thing isn't a metaphor for my future writing career.*

The first wizard started to speak. "Welcome to the WGA."

It was Billy Ray, the esteemed screenwriter of *Captain Phillips* and *The Hunger Games*. At the time, he was best known for *The Color of Night* starring Bruce Willis, a film that by today's standards has aged like milk left in a hot car.

Billy Ray gave us a pep talk like we were about to play our rival high school in the big game. As I scanned the room, I realized there were maybe 150 new members present. I felt pretty good to be included in this small cadre of writers, all excited and eager to join the one and only writers' union that means anything in film and TV.

Billy Ray continued, "You are now a professional writer. You had about a five times better chance of hearing your name read at the Major League Baseball draft this year than getting invited to join the WGA. Approximately 1,500 players are drafted into Major League Baseball every year. Approximately 300 new members are admitted into the WGA every year."

Okay, cool. I chuckled to myself as I looked around the room. I wasn't too sure how many of these newbie screen and TV writers watched sports. Probably even fewer could throw a baseball. *But hey, we made it.*

The next speaker stood up to fill us with career advice. It was David Goyer, who had written the *Blade* films and worked with Christopher Nolan on the *Dark Knight* trilogy. The only part of his speech I remember is him telling us something about how awesome residuals are and how we'll be grateful we joined the WGA when we start getting $80,000 checks in the mail.

I'm still waiting for that $80,000 check to this day. Mine are more like $80 if I'm lucky. Sometimes $800 if the universe is feeling generous.

While I appreciated the motivational speeches, what I learned most of all that day was that every writer has their own career path.

Screen and TV writing careers are very reflective of society. The top two percent make astronomical amounts of money, get the best paying jobs and have more projects than they know what to do with. Next on the totem pole is a swath of working writers who get paid well but have to be constantly looking for gigs and opportunities. Then there are the non-working members of the WGA, which I've heard is approximately 50 percent of the 12,000 members. With the current contraction of streamer content and the spread of AI, that number will probably rise.

What you do with your career is completely up to you. I've never had the opportunity to write a film like *The Batman* or *The Hunger Games*. But I have been lucky enough to write scripts for a living for almost 20 years. I can't complain.

Here's the truth: Joining the WGA won't get you work. They don't function as your agent or manager. They don't send your scripts out to producers. They don't make phone calls on your behalf telling people you're brilliant.

What they do is make sure certain things are guaranteed in your contract. If the producers, studio or streamer doesn't follow those guarantees, the Guild does the dirty work of making sure you're not screwed over.

In theory, anyway.

Almost all TV work is WGA. If you get hired on a TV show as a staff writer, you don't have a choice—you have to join. Almost all studios and streamers are WGA signatories.

What does that mean?

A WGA signatory company is any production company, studio, network, streaming platform or producer that has signed the Writers Guild of America's Minimum Basic Agreement. By signing the MBA, the company agrees to abide by all of the Guild's rules when hiring writers. This includes paying Guild minimum rates, providing residuals, contributing to the Guild's health and pension plans and following Guild credit determination procedures.

Sounds great, right? Professional protections. Fair compensation. The American Dream wrapped in contract language.

Here's where it gets messy. Many producers and financiers don't want to be WGA signatories because it means they have to sign a financial guarantee to pay residuals and other expenses. Many small films don't want to pay residuals, pension and health contributions. They may not want to work with a WGA writer at all and may pass on any project written by a WGA-represented writer altogether.

In other words, the protections that are supposed to help you can actually prevent your scripts from getting made on certain smaller productions.

When we worked out the deal for *Tokarev* (aka *Rage*), I knew the film was going to make a lot in terms of residuals—foreign sales, streaming, cable and the whole buffet of ancillary markets. My one stipulation was that it had to be WGA so I could join the Guild and get paid those residuals from every market worldwide.

This seemed reasonable. Professional even.

A few weeks before filming started, the producers called and said they couldn't produce the film as WGA. If I didn't agree to make it non-WGA, they wouldn't be able to make the film at all.

By this time, I'd learned a lot about how films are made and financed. More importantly, I'd learned about leverage. They had more to lose at this point financially than I did. They had Nicolas Cage attached. They had locations scouted. They had money committed. Walking away would cost them a fortune.

My response: "Fuck off. Don't make the film, then." And I hung up the phone.

An hour later they called back. "Okay, we'll make it WGA."

PSA: Bluffing only works when you know the other side has more to lose than you do.

The movie was wildly successful and made a ton of money. It played in theaters internationally, sold to every cable network you've heard of (and several you haven't) and landed on streaming platforms worldwide.

And yet the producer and financier decided to try to find a loophole in the WGA paperwork to avoid paying residuals.

Even though they'd made so much money off our film that they were racing into production with Nicolas Cage on another $10 million project. Even though they were clearly flush with cash. Even though the contract was crystal clear about what they owed me.

It took years of arbitration with the WGA legal team and battle after battle to get paid what I was owed at the time. A lot of shitty emails. Name-calling from both the producer and financier. Threats. Excuses. The usual dance done by people who have money and don't want to part with it.

Cut to a decade later. *Rage* is on streaming platforms Tubi, Plex, Philo, Fandango, YouTube, Apple TV and Amazon Prime—just in the US alone. Worldwide, it's probably on hundreds of streamers.

The film is everywhere, still generating a lot of money.

How much have I been paid in residuals over the last 10 years since the initial payment I had to fight so hard to get?

Not one fucking dollar.

CHAPTER 19

LIVE AND LET DEI

I RECENTLY WENT to a party where I was introduced to a TV showrunner and his wife, also a showrunner and creator. Between them, they'd helmed several successful TV shows for the last 25 years—a genuine industry power couple.

Since it's LA, the conversation inevitably turned to "What do you do?" This is the city's favorite question, though it can often really mean "Are you worth talking to?"

I explained that I'm a writer who's worked mostly in feature films with budgets between $2 million and $10 million. Since they were TV people, I added that I'd sold a show to ABC and been hired to write several pilots. But, I explained, once I had serious momentum in television—peaking around 2016—all that career velocity hit a wall. I was told by almost everyone, including my agent, that I couldn't be considered for TV jobs because I was a straight white male.

The female showrunner's response was, "Oh, that's over now."

Four words, delivered with the casual indifference of someone commenting on the weather.

I didn't know how to process her statement. Was it a

victory where the quiet part that was only whispered before is now being said out loud? Or was it a devastating loss that two decades of momentum had evaporated because of my demographic profile? The nonchalance of her delivery was perhaps the most shocking part. Did she mean the industry's approach had been misguided? Or was it simply that it hadn't impacted her, so who cares?

The quiet part was that if you were white and straight, no matter what your qualifications were, for the most part you were not going to get hired in this new world of DEI initiatives. It was time to push aside an entire group of writers based on race.

I don't know how many times I heard the term "Male and pale is stale."

I remember vividly when this attitude started. I'd been in hundreds of meetings at studios, streamers and networks over the years. Race, gender, sexuality—none of those things seemed to matter in the evaluation process. If you could do the job, you got hired. At least that's how I'd always experienced it.

On the first indie film I produced in the late '90s, I advocated hiring a female director of photography—a rarity at the time. She did excellent work. The first film I directed had a cast of four: two men, two women. Of the two men, one was white and one was Black. I hired the best person for each role without consulting any checklist.

I may have been naive about how the world was shifting. I'd hired many people as a producer and always focused on competence over demographics. For reasons I'm still trying to understand, the rest of the industry started feeling differently.

In 2021, I had an action script that a successful network showrunner wanted to direct. That's the peculiar thing about the TV industry—everyone in television wants to make a feature film, while most feature writers recognize the instability of that world and want to break into TV for the security it provides.

This showrunner asked me to do several free rewrites on the script. I obliged, thinking perhaps he'd return the favor and get me a writing job on his massively successful show. He never did. But in one conversation, I mentioned a female director I knew who was making her first small indie feature. He instantly replied, "Send me her demo. I need to hire some female directors."

In other words, he wanted to direct a script I wrote, so obviously he respected my writing. But when I asked about a writing gig, he said he couldn't help because I was a white guy. Yet he's willing to hire a female director with no credits, someone he's never met?

For several years, it was like this.

Much of it was fueled by the streaming wars. They needed content, and fast. Everyone wanted to become the next Netflix: Paramount Plus, Max and Amazon. It was a race for market share—not quality content but market share, that beautiful metric that makes executives salivate and artists weep.

Sometime before this shift, in early 2017, I was pitching a TV show with a well-known producer at Netflix's fancy new offices. I was amazed at the scale of the place—you want coffee? There's a massive coffee bar in the lobby. You want a sandwich? Done. As we waited to pitch our sci-fi concept, I said to the producer, "I can't believe how much they spent on their lobby. This is crazy."

We'd just pitched the same show to several companies housed in studio bungalows from the 1930s. If you've ever been to a bungalow office at a studio, they're surprisingly unimpressive: always a bookshelf filled with old scripts, decade-old cracks in the walls, and one or two framed posters from previous productions. Those places looked nothing like the glitter and glamour of the Netflix waiting area.

The producer looked at me and stated flatly, "This isn't an entertainment company. It's a tech company. They think like a tech company; they do business like a tech company—not like an old-school entertainment company like Warner's or Paramount. They're racing for market share, and that's all that matters."

Over time, his words proved prophetic.

My personal opinion: The streaming wars, mixed with the 2016 election, COVID and the catastrophe that was the first half of the 2020s, created a perfect storm where identity became the key factor in the film and TV business—above creativity and profitability. It became the only thing that seemed to matter most. TV shows made for very niche markets were green-lit across the board. Netflix and its competitors had turned on the money hose in their battle for market share.

They weren't making content for a wider audience. It became the era of boutique television, where programs could appeal to a sliver of demographics. And from what I saw, every idea now had to be filtered through some ideological lens. Every pitch, every show and every writer had to take on a cause or agenda, shining a light on something that needed to change in society.

I heard very little talk about entertaining people. About making anything that was...fun. Even Star Wars and Marvel— the stories I grew up on as a kid, the things that drove me into this business—had become unrecognizable to me.

For a moment, I thought: *Why am I doing this anymore?*

Everyone in the film business supported diversity in principle, but that started to mean hiring writers who weren't experienced enough to keep up with the demands of the job.

The misconception is that you only need talent to be a

successful working writer. You do need talent, but you also need experience—the ability to pull tricks from your bag when facing a deadline. You need to be able to lean on the development of your craft as a professional to get across the finish line. The raw and uninitiated haven't developed those skills yet.

And that's what happened repeatedly. I heard stories of first-time staff writers not delivering episodes on time, forcing a scramble where seasoned writers had to write an episode over a weekend on top of their own responsibilities. The kicker? When the inexperienced writer didn't deliver on their episode, and it was all hands on deck in a last-ditch effort to keep the show on schedule, that writer still received credit, pay and residuals—either because it was contractually obligated or senior staff wanted to keep the peace with their corporate overlords.

I attended the WGA's meeting to discuss internal issues before the 2023 strike. To enter, I had to show my ID, prove I'd been vaccinated against COVID and had received the booster, then navigate through metal detectors. Inside were about 2,500 people, and I'd estimate half were still wearing masks.

I'd been to several of these events over the years. They happen every three years before the WGA votes on a new Minimum Basic Agreement (which spells out the rules for union members for the next three years). Usually at these events, it's people complaining about two things: pay and residuals.

This time was different. Young writers, one by one, approached the microphone asking questions about how the WGA would guarantee them jobs. Questions about diversity, diversity and more diversity. "How come I'm not a showrunner yet? I sold two pilots but now can't find work. How can you make sure I get more work?"

This went on for hours.

It hit me: These new writers who'd recently been hired on TV shows had a relatively easy path getting there. Hiring based on gender, sexual orientation or race had accelerated their arrival. Because their path had been so easy, they didn't understand that once you get there, it's a grind. They didn't know that making a living as a screenwriter or TV writer is a lifetime hustle.

A veteran writer standing next to me in the back rolled his eyes every time someone new approached the microphone.

For someone who believes the best way to navigate a writing career is to understand the business, this night was difficult to watch.

But then the strikes happened, and the streaming wars essentially ended with companies consolidating or closing shop. Netflix had won. Reality set in again, and the only color that mattered was green—the color of money.

Entertaining people and the financial bottom line re-emerged as the drivers of content. Not identity, not politics, not race and especially not ideology.

As a straight white guy, I'm not asking for sympathy. I rolled with this mess and managed to keep working. I'm fortunate that most of my experience has been in indie films, where margins are tight and financiers don't have the luxury of making statements with their hiring decisions. They need to make a profit and don't care about your color or orientation—as long as the film makes money, that's all that matters. So even though TV was out, I had enough connections to keep working in film.

If the diversity initiative forced across film and TV had been a smashing success that reinvigorated the industry socially, creatively and financially, there would be no reason to pull back. It would have ushered in a new, profitable golden age of film and TV.

On where, you wouldn't hear one-time successful showrunners, who currently have no projects in development, say...

"Oh, that's over now."

CHAPTER 20

EX MACHINA (FOR SCREENWRITERS)

I'VE BEEN HEARING it a lot lately from professional screenwriters, always delivered with the kind of self-righteous conviction usually reserved for people explaining their CrossFit routine:

"Using AI isn't real writing. It isn't true filmmaking. I'll never use that shit."

That's great. Congratulations on your principles. But tell me something—do you also still use a typewriter? Do you eschew internet research in favor of facts found only in books buried deep in the confusing labyrinth of a library? Do you hand-deliver your scripts via horseback?

Of course you don't. Because that would be fucking absurd.

If you have a romantic notion of writing in the middle of the night with a cigarette dangling from your lips and a glass of whiskey at your side while inspiration strikes like lightning— that's your prerogative. Light that Marlboro. Pour that Jameson. Wait for the muse.

But in the real world of screenwriting—and probably even more so for TV writers grinding episode by episode—output and deadlines are what separate the professionals from the amateurs.

Nobody cares how pure your creative process is if you can't deliver on time.

I've started using AI for writing scripts, and what it can do is both terrifying and honestly, kind of hilarious. I look at AI as the writing assistant I could never afford—the one who doesn't need health insurance, doesn't take lunch breaks and never complains about working weekends.

But here's the thing people don't understand: You need to know what to ask it to help you with. AI isn't magic. It's a tool for productivity, and like any tool, it's only as good as the person wielding it.

Think of it this way: Anyone can't just climb into a cockpit, tell the autopilot to take off and expect to end up safely in Cabo. You need someone with experience who knows how to fly a plane to input the information correctly. The autopilot doesn't replace the pilot—it makes the pilot more effective.

Same goes for AI in screenwriting. It doesn't replace the writer. It makes the writer more productive. If you don't understand story structure, character development and dramatic tension, AI will just help you write garbage faster.

And it's not just writing. Visuals are moving at the speed of light. AI-generated imagery is evolving so rapidly that sooner than later, filmmakers will have an entire studio inside their laptop. Filmmaking will be democratized more than ever before.

So what does that mean for the burgeoning screenwriter?

It opens up a multitude of opportunities for writers who actually understand the craft of story, character and structure. In a world where anyone can just make something that looks professional, the most important skill will be screenwriting.

I would rather watch *Swingers* again than sit through *The Rise of Skywalker*.

Swingers is a technological disaster: bad lighting, half-assed camera moves and unwieldy locations shot with borrowed equipment. *Rise of Skywalker* is a technological marvel, every frame a masterpiece of digital wizardry and VFX artistry.

But *Swingers* has great dialogue, relatable characters and heart. You forgive the filmmaking limitations because you're invested in the story. *Rise of Skywalker* is the opposite—all spectacle, no soul. It's like eating a beautifully plated dish that tastes like cardboard.

Technology never trumps story. Ever.

Who's seen *Clerks*? A lot of people. It's a cultural touchstone, quoted and referenced decades later. *47 Ronin*? That $175 million Keanu Reeves samurai fantasy with cutting-edge CGI? Nobody.

"But are there going to be jobs in the future?"

Yes. Just different ones.

I've been around the film business for over 30 years, and I've seen a lot change. Every three to five years, there's a massive shift in the business side of things. VHS money came and then went. Then DVD money—which was glorious while it lasted. Then streamers changed everything. Now budgets are shrinking and TV content is contracting more than ever.

Every time the industry shifts, you need to shift with it. The people who survive are the ones who adapt. The ones who cling to "how things used to be" become cautionary tales told at dive bars in Los Feliz.

That's what this whole book is about.

Understand the business as much as the creative side of things, and you'll always have an upper hand in getting your screenwriting career off the ground. Know how deals work. Understand what producers need. Learn the new tools. Adapt to the changing landscape.

The future doesn't care about your nostalgia for the golden age of Hollywood. The future doesn't give a shit about your principles regarding AI or your romantic notions about the purity of the creative process.

The future is here. You can either learn to navigate it, or you can stand on the shore complaining about how the ocean used to be better.

Your choice.

Trust me, if a kid from a dirt town with a dodgy education who still doesn't know what an adverb is can make a living at this, so can you.

The rest of the book is my guide to understanding more of the nuts and bolts of being a working screenwriter.

CHAPTER 21

THE COLOR OF MONEY (AND A FEW OTHER THINGS YOU NEED TO KNOW)

THE BUSINESS SIDE of screenwriting is messy, unglamorous and necessary. I've pulled together the stuff nobody wants to talk about at cocktail parties but everyone needs to know before they get their ass handed to them.

Here's what we're covering:

Option/Purchase Agreements – The deal that might make you rich, or at least pay your rent

Chain of Title – Proof you actually own what you're selling (crucial, boring and non-negotiable)

Why Agents and Managers Don't Want Your Script – It's not personal. Well, maybe it is. Either way, you should know why

WGA Versus Non-WGA – Union protection or wild west freelancing—both have their costs

TV Pitch Template – Straight from Lionsgate TV, because stealing from the best is just good strategy

Sample Agreements – The actual paperwork, so you know what you're signing before the lawyers get involved

WHAT IS AN OPTION/PURCHASE AGREEMENT?

An option/purchase agreement is the legal foundation of how a script becomes a film. It's the bridge between your Final Draft file and the actual production. Here's the basic trajectory: You write a script. A producer or studio reads it and wants to make it. But here's the thing—they don't want to pay full price until they know they can actually get the film made. That's where the option comes in.

HOW OPTIONS WORK

An option gives a producer the exclusive right to purchase your screenplay within a set period of time—usually between 18 months and two years, though this is negotiable. Think of it as a reservation fee on your script.

Here's a typical scenario: A producer pays you $1,000 to option your screenplay for 18 months. The agreed-upon purchase price is $50,000. During those 18 months, you cannot sell the script to anyone else. The producer essentially controls the rights, but they cannot make the film until they pay you the full $50,000 purchase price.

Important note: unless you're a member of the Writers Guild of America (WGA), there are no minimum amounts. The option fee and purchase price can be literally anything you negotiate. One-dollar options are surprisingly common, especially for first-time writers or when working with independent producers with limited development funds.

OPTION EXTENSIONS

Many option agreements include provisions for extensions. After the initial 18-month period expires, the producer may have the right to extend the option for an additional period—say, another 12 or 18 months—by paying you an additional fee (perhaps another $1,000).

This extension can work in two ways:

Automatic extension right: The producer has the unilateral right to extend by paying the additional fee

Mutual agreement: Both parties must agree to the extension

Which structure you agree to should be determined at the beginning and clearly stated in your contract. Generally, if a producer is making genuine progress toward getting your film made, extensions are in everyone's interest. If they're sitting on your script doing nothing, you'll want it back.

WHEN YOU GET PAID

Let's say lightning strikes—your producer gets the film financed. When do you actually see your money?

Industry standard dictates that you're paid the full purchase price on the first day of principal photography. Not during pre-production, but on the actual first day of shooting. This protects both you and the producer. If the film falls apart during pre-production (which happens more often than anyone likes to admit), the producer hasn't paid for a script they can't use, and you get your rights back when the option expires. You can then option it again to someone else (or the same producer).

OTHER CRITICAL DEAL POINTS

The option fee and purchase price are just the beginning. Here are other essential elements you need to negotiate and include in your option agreement:

Credit: Will you receive "Written by" credit? "Story by" credit? What happens if the producer brings in other writers for rewrites? Screen credit can affect your residuals, your reputation and your career trajectory. For WGA members, credit is determined by WGA rules through arbitration if necessary. For non-WGA writers, whatever is in your contract is what you get —so make sure it's spelled out clearly.

Sequels and remakes: If your film becomes the next big franchise, you want to be compensated. Your agreement should specify whether you'll be paid for sequels, remakes or reboots, and how much. Do you have the right of first refusal to write the sequel? Are you paid a percentage of your original fee? These rights are often referred to as "separated rights" in WGA contracts, but can be part of any contract.

Television and streaming adaptations: In today's market, a successful film sometimes becomes a TV series. Your option should address whether a TV show, limited series or streaming series based on your screenplay requires additional compensation. Do you receive consulting producer fees? Royalties per episode? Will you have any creative involvement?

Backend participation: Also called "net profits" or "gross participation," this is your percentage of the film's profits after it's released. Fair warning: Net profits are notoriously difficult to see because of Hollywood accounting practices.

Reversion of rights: What happens if the option expires and the producer hasn't made the film? Your agreement should clearly state that all rights revert back to you.

A WORD ON LEGAL REPRESENTATION

This is not legal advice. Seriously—hire an entertainment attorney if you can possibly afford one. Entertainment law is highly specialized, and a general practice lawyer or real estate attorney won't know the industry standards and potential pitfalls.

If you absolutely cannot afford an attorney, at minimum:

- Download and study the WGA's standard contracts (even if you're not a member, they're instructive).
- Research comparable deals in your situation (debut writer, independent producer, or other).
- Never sign anything under pressure.
- Have someone with industry experience review the agreement.

Good entertainment attorneys will pay for themselves many times over by catching problematic clauses and negotiating better terms.

THE SHOPPING AGREEMENT VERSUS AN OPTION

A shopping agreement in the film and TV world is a short-term deal that allows a producer, agent or manager to "shop" your screenplay or concept to studios, financiers or networks without owning it outright.

It's essentially a temporary option in which you, the writer or rights holder, grant the producer permission to present or pitch the project to potential buyers. You still retain ownership of the screenplay. The producer's goal is to set up the project—either by selling it or attaching financing—at which point a formal option-purchase or development deal is negotiated. These agreements can be for weeks or months.

Typically, no payment is made up front, unlike a traditional option. The producer often has exclusive rights to shop the material during the term. If the project is successfully set up, the producer then receives a producing fee or credit as part of the larger deal. If the term expires and the project isn't sold or financed, the rights revert to you automatically.

Legally, a shopping agreement can hold up if it's properly drafted, but it's limited in scope. It should clearly state that the producer has no ownership or underlying rights, only permission to shop the project. Courts generally recognize these agreements as enforceable licensing contracts, though vague wording can cause disputes—for instance, if a producer later claims implied rights or continuing attachments.

In short, a shopping agreement is a low-risk, low-cost way to let someone try to get your project set up, as long as it's clear and time-limited. Writers should make sure the term is short, that rights automatically revert once it expires and that no clause gives the producer perpetual attachment or ownership.

THE REALITY CHECK

Most optioned screenplays never get made. That's not pessimism—it's statistics. A producer might option dozens of scripts and only get one or two into production. This is why producers want options rather than outright purchases, and why you shouldn't quit your day job just because someone optioned your script.

But an option is still meaningful. It means a professional believed in your work enough to invest in it. It gives you a legitimate credit to put in your query letters. And it means you're in the game.

Just remember: They optioned your script. They haven't bought it. Not really. Not yet.

WHAT IS CHAIN OF TITLE?

Chain of title is the complete, documented history of ownership and rights to your screenplay. It's the paper trail that proves you have the legal right to sell or option your script, and that no one else can suddenly claim they own it.

Think of it like the title to your car. Before someone buys your car, they want proof that you actually own it and have the right to sell. The same principle applies to your screenplay, except the stakes can be much higher: A studio isn't going to invest millions of dollars in a film if there's any question about who owns the underlying material.

A broken or incomplete chain of title can kill a deal instantly—no matter how brilliant your script is.

THE ESSENTIAL DOCUMENTS

Building a solid chain of title requires several key documents. Let's walk through each one:

Certificate of Authorship

A Certificate of Authorship is your sworn statement that you wrote the screenplay. It typically includes:

- Your legal name and contact information
- The title of the screenplay
- A statement that you are the sole author (or one of multiple authors)
- Confirmation that the work is original or, if based on underlying material, that you have the rights to that material
- The date the screenplay was completed
- Your signature, ideally notarized

This document establishes you as the creator. Even if you're the only writer, you should create this document and keep it with your script files. It's simple to make now and invaluable later.

Copyright Registration

Here's where many writers get confused: Your screenplay is automatically copyrighted the moment you write it. You don't need to register it for copyright protection to exist.

However, registering your copyright with the U.S. Copyright Office provides significant legal advantages:

- **Public record of ownership:** Official government documentation that you created the work on a specific date.
- **Legal standing:** You must have a registered copyright to file an infringement lawsuit in federal court.
- **Statutory damages:** Registration allows you to claim statutory damages and attorney's fees in infringement cases, rather than just actual damages (which can be hard to prove).
- **Presumption of validity:** If registered within five years of publication, the registration establishes prima facie evidence of validity.

Registration costs around $65 online and takes several weeks to process, though you have protection from the date you file, not the date the certificate arrives. This is money well spent.

Important distinction: Registering with the WGA is not the same as copyright registration. WGA registration is useful for establishing a completion date and can help in disputes, but it's not a legal copyright registration and doesn't provide the same protections or legal standing.

Assignment or Transfer of Copyright

When a producer options or purchases your screenplay, they need you to either transfer the copyright or grant them specific rights. This is done through an Assignment of Copyright document, also called a Transfer of Copyright.

This document should specify:

- What rights are being transferred (often "all right, title, and interest")
- Whether the transfer is conditional (such as "upon payment of the purchase price")
- What territory the rights cover (usually worldwide)
- What media the rights cover (theatrical, television, streaming or other)
- The term of the transfer (in perpetuity is standard for purchases)

For an option, you're typically not transferring the copyright yet—you're granting the exclusive right to purchase it later. The actual transfer happens when they exercise the option and pay you the purchase price, not before.

Why Documentation Matters Even More for Co-Writers

If you wrote your screenplay with one or more collaborators, your chain of title becomes exponentially more complex—and proper documentation becomes absolutely critical.

The Collaboration Agreement

Before you write a single word with a co-writer, you should have a written collaboration agreement that specifies:

- **Ownership percentages:** Who owns what percentage of the screenplay? 50/50? 60/40? This affects how option and purchase money gets split and who has control over decisions.
- **Credit determination:** How will the writing credit read? This should align with your ownership split and actual contributions.

- **Decision-making:** How will decisions be made about optioning or selling the script? Must all writers agree? Does majority rule?
- **Dispute resolution:** What happens if you disagree about whether to accept an offer?
- **Solo exploitation:** Can one writer use the characters or story in other projects without the other writer's permission?
- **What happens if someone dies:** Morbid but necessary—what happens to that writer's share and decision-making power?

Without this agreement in writing, you're inviting disaster. Imagine: A producer wants to option your script. Your co-writer, who contributed 20 percent of the work but legally owns 50 percent because you never documented the arrangement, refuses to sign unless they get 50 percent of the money. Your deal collapses.

Or worse: You sell your script. Your co-writer sues, claiming they were never properly compensated. The studio has to halt production while the lawsuit plays out. You might get sued too. Everyone loses.

Documentation for Multi-Writer Projects

For a screenplay with multiple writers, your chain of title package should include:

- Individual Certificates of Authorship from each writer, stating what they contributed
- The collaboration agreement, establishing ownership splits and rights
- Joint copyright registration listing all authors

- Consent and agreement documents from all writers, agreeing to the option or sale
- Individual Assignments of Copyright from each writer to the purchasing entity

Yes, it's a lot of paperwork. But it's infinitely easier to gather these signatures when everyone's happy and excited about the project than when someone feels they're getting screwed out of money or credit.

Based on a True Story: Underlying Rights

If your screenplay is based on someone else's work—a novel, a life story, a magazine article, a comic book or even a tweet—you need documentation proving you have the rights to adapt that material.

This includes:

- Option or purchase agreement for the underlying work
- Life rights agreement if based on a real person's story
- Assignment of rights from the original creator
- Public domain research, with documentation to prove it, if you're claiming the source material is in the public domain

Even if you based your script on your own novel, you should have documentation establishing that you wrote the novel and own those rights. If you published the novel through a publisher, check your publishing contract—you may have granted them certain film or TV rights.

The Special Hell of "Based on an Idea By"

Here's a nightmare scenario: You write a screenplay. Someone claims they told you the idea at a party three years ago and they deserve credit and money.

This happens more often than you'd think. Protect yourself:

- Document everything: If someone pitches you an idea and you want to write it, get them to sign a simple agreement establishing what they contributed and what they'll receive—in credit, money or both.
- Keep all emails and messages showing the development of the idea and who contributed what.
- Be careful about "idea people." If someone just says, "You should write a movie about X," that's not something you typically owe them for—ideas aren't copyrightable. But if they provide detailed character descriptions, plot points and story structure, that's potentially a protectable contribution.

Keeping Your Chain of Title Clean

To maintain bulletproof documentation, here's what you should do from the start:

- Create a Certificate of Authorship as soon as you finish your script.
- Register your copyright ASAP.
- If working with co-writers, execute a collaboration agreement before writing.

- Keep drafts with dates to show the evolution of the work.

Ongoing maintenance:

- Store all documents in both physical and digital form.
- Use cloud storage with backup for digital files.
- Keep a master folder for each screenplay with all related documents.
- Update certificates if you do major rewrites that substantially change the story.

Before any deal:

- Gather all chain of title documents before you start negotiating.
- Have them reviewed by an entertainment attorney.
- Get signatures from any co-writers or underlying rights holders.
- Make sure everything is notarized where appropriate.

What Happens If Your Chain of Title Has Problems

Let's say you're in the middle of negotiating an option and you realize you never got your co-writer to sign a collaboration agreement. What now?

Don't panic, but act quickly:

- **Be honest with your potential buyer:** Disclose the issue immediately. Trying to hide it will only make things worse.
- **Fix it if possible:** Go to your co-writer and get the proper documentation done now. Yes, they now have leverage, but a late agreement is better than no agreement.
- **Get legal help:** An entertainment attorney can help you navigate the situation and may be able to structure the deal to minimize risk.
- **Be prepared to walk away:** If your co-writer makes unreasonable demands, you may need to let this opportunity pass and get everything properly documented before the next one.

Some problems can't be fixed. If you adapted a novel without getting the rights, there's no deal to be made until you secure those rights—which may now be impossible or prohibitively expensive.

A Word on Legal Representation (Yes, Again)

This is not legal advice. Chain of title issues are complex and state-specific. An entertainment attorney can:

- Review your documentation and identify gaps
- Draft proper collaboration agreements
- Handle copyright registrations
- Structure assignments to protect both you and the buyer
- Resolve disputes with co-writers or underlying rights holders

The cost of an attorney is small compared to losing a deal or getting sued because your documentation was insufficient.

The Bottom Line

Chain of title documentation feels like tedious paperwork when you'd rather be writing. But it's the foundation that turns your screenplay into a professional commodity.

Start building your chain of title the day you start writing. Keep meticulous records. Get everything in writing. Have co-writers sign agreements before you collaborate, not after. The best screenplay in the world is worthless if you can't prove you have the right to sell it.

Your paper trail is as important as your plot points. Treat it that way.

CHAPTER 22
WHY NOBODY WILL READ YOUR SCRIPT (AND IT'S NOT PERSONAL)

YOU'VE WRITTEN A KILLER SCREENPLAY. You send it to a major agency. You get a form letter back: "We do not accept unsolicited material."

You're confused: *Isn't finding new writers literally their job? Why won't they even look at it?*

The answer isn't about the quality of your script. It's about something much more mundane and expensive: legal liability.

THE EXPOSURE PROBLEM

Here's the scenario that keeps agents, managers, producers and studio executives up at night:

They read your zombie apocalypse script in January. In March, their client sells a zombie apocalypse script to a studio. In April, you see the trade announcement. In May, your lawyer sends them a cease-and-desist letter claiming they stole your idea.

Now they're in litigation. Even if your script and theirs have nothing in common beyond "zombies and apocalypse," they have to:

- Hire attorneys (expensive)
- Produce documents for discovery (expensive and time-consuming)
- Possibly go through depositions (expensive and humiliating)
- Potentially go to trial (catastrophically expensive)
- Deal with negative publicity (priceless, in the worst way)

Even if they win the lawsuit and prove they never stole anything, they've spent tens or hundreds of thousands of dollars and countless hours defending themselves.

This is called "exposure," and it's why the entertainment industry has developed an immune system that rejects unsolicited material like a body rejects a foreign organ.

IT HAPPENS MORE THAN YOU THINK

You might think, "But I'm not the kind of person who would sue frivolously." That's great. Unfortunately, they don't know that. And they've been burned before.

Consider these scenarios:

- **The coincidence problem:** There are only so many basic story concepts. "Cop partnered with unlikely partner to solve crime" has been done hundreds of times. "Regular person discovers they have special powers" is a genre unto itself. Two writers can independently create similar scripts without ever having seen each other's work. But try explaining that to a jury.

- **The idea person:** Someone pitches a vague idea to a producer at a party, like "What if dinosaurs came back?" Later, the producer develops a completely different dinosaur project with a professional writer. The idea person sues, claiming they own the concept. The producer has to prove they came up with their version independently.
- **The prior submission:** An agency receives possibly thousands of scripts a month. An assistant reads your script in the slush pile and passes. Two years later, the agency packages a similar film. You sue, claiming they stole your concept. The agency has to locate whoever read your script years ago, reconstruct what happened and prove there was no connection.
- **The false memory:** Someone genuinely but incorrectly remembers sharing their script with a producer who later makes a similar film. They're not lying—they truly believe they sent it. But they didn't.

These situations are common enough that the entire industry has adopted defensive policies to prevent them.

THE RELEASE FORM: LEGAL PROTECTION (SORT OF)

When an agent, manager or producer is willing to read material from someone they don't know, they typically require a submission release form (also called a "release agreement" or "unsolicited material release").

This document usually includes the following points:

- **Similar material:** They may have already read, developed or purchased similar material, and you can't sue them for that.
- **Independent development:** They may independently develop similar ideas, and that's not theft.
- **No implied contract:** Sending them your script doesn't create any obligation on their part.
- **Ideas aren't protectable:** General concepts and ideas aren't copyrightable, only specific expression.
- **No compensation:** They're reading your script as a courtesy and owe you nothing unless they explicitly option or purchase it.
- **Waiver of claims:** You're waiving your right to sue them for idea theft (though not for actual copyright infringement).

Some release forms are reasonable. Others are incredibly one-sided, essentially asking you to give up all your rights just for the privilege of having your script read.

Should you sign them? That's a personal decision. Many professionals refuse on principle. Others sign selectively. An entertainment attorney can review specific release forms and advise you.

WHY ESTABLISHED WRITERS DON'T HAVE THIS PROBLEM

If you're represented by a major agency or have a track record, your submissions aren't "unsolicited." You're part of the system, and here's why that matters:

- **Relationships and reputation:** Established writers have relationships with industry professionals. They have a track record of not suing if there are similar ideas—they understand that's just part of the business. Nobody wants to risk their reputation by stealing from or suing someone they know and work with regularly.
- **Guild protection:** WGA members have access to arbitration and the Guild's legal resources if disputes arise. This creates a deterrent against theft.
- **Paper trails:** When material comes through agents or managers, there's documentation of who sent what to whom and when. This makes fraudulent claims much harder.
- **Less paranoia needed:** When a producer knows the writer, is familiar with their work and has a professional relationship with them, there's trust. They're not worried about frivolous lawsuits because they can pick up the phone and have a conversation.

This creates an unfortunate Catch-22: You need industry connections to get your script read safely, but you need to get your script read to build industry connections.

HOW IDEAS ACTUALLY GET STOLEN (AND HOW THEY DON'T)

Let's be clear about something: Theft does happen in Hollywood. But it rarely happens the way emerging writers fear.

How ideas *don't* get stolen:

- An agent reads your script and secretly passes the concept to a client.
- A producer reads your zombie script and immediately makes their own zombie movie.
- Someone reads your logline and develops an entire film from it.

How theft actually occurs:

- A writer is hired to develop something, does substantial work and is then cut out without proper credit or compensation.
- Underlying rights (to a book, article or life story) are used without proper payment or permission.
- A treatment or detailed pitch is used without crediting the originator.
- A finished script is produced with minimal changes but the writer is denied credit.

Real theft involves specific, protectable expression—not general concepts. And it usually happens within existing professional relationships, not from cold submissions.

WHAT THIS MEANS FOR EMERGING WRITERS

So if agents and managers won't read unsolicited material, how do you break in?

Legitimate paths:

- **Referrals:** Get someone they know to recommend you. This is why networking matters.

- **Contests and fellowships:** Win or place in legitimate screenwriting competitions. This provides third-party validation and gets you noticed.
- **Query letters:** Some representatives will read a one-page query letter describing your script. If they're interested, they'll request the script, making it "solicited."
- **Manager first:** Managers are generally more open to new writers than agents. Land a manager who can then get your work to agents and producers.
- **Produce it yourself:** Make your own short film or web series. Prove you can execute.
- **Write for existing content:** Start in TV writers' rooms, write for a web series or work your way up through more accessible entry points.

What doesn't work:

- Dropping your script off at agency reception desks (it will go straight to the trash)
- Cold-emailing scripts to agents (they won't open the attachment)
- Confronting agents at industry events and pitching aggressively (you'll get blacklisted)

PROTECTING YOURSELF

While you're navigating this system, here's how to protect your own work:

- Copyright everything, as discussed.

- Keep records of who you sent your script to and when. Save all correspondence. If you do sign a release form, keep a copy.
- Be strategic about sharing: Don't post your entire script publicly online where anyone can access it.
- Understand what's protectable: Your specific dialogue, characters, scenes and plot details are protected. The general concept ("a heist movie") is not. Neither are standard genre elements (the "wise mentor" in a martial arts movie).
- Don't pitch prematurely and tell everyone your idea before you've written it. Once you've written the script, your expression of the idea is protected. Before that, you have nothing protectable.

THE PARANOIA BALANCE

There's a balance to strike here. Too little caution, and people might genuinely take advantage of you. Too much paranoia, and you'll never get anywhere because you won't let anyone read your work.

Some perspective:

- The vast majority of industry professionals are honest and aren't trying to steal your work.
- Your script is probably not as similar to their project as you think it is.
- Your ability to execute ideas matters more than any single idea.

THE UNCOMFORTABLE TRUTH

Here's what nobody wants to tell emerging writers: The system is designed to keep you out until you've proven yourself through other means. "No unsolicited submissions" isn't about the quality of your work—it's about legal risk management.

This isn't fair. It makes breaking in much harder than it should be. But it's the reality.

Your job is to find the cracks in the wall: contests, referrals, fellowships, managers who specialize in developing new talent and opportunities to network at the right events. Most importantly, concentrate on creating strong content that showcases your abilities.

The good news is that once you're in—once you have representation, credits and relationships—this particular problem goes away. The bad news is that getting to that point requires navigating a system that's specifically designed to keep unknowns at arm's length.

A FINAL WORD ON RELEASE FORMS

If you're asked to sign a submission release form, here are some red flags to watch for:

- **Unlimited rights grant:** Language suggesting you're giving them rights to your material just by submitting it
- **No recourse for actual theft:** Language that prevents you from suing even for legitimate copyright infringement
- **Perpetual NDA:** Language preventing you from ever discussing your submission or their response

- **Assignment of rights:** Any suggestion that you're transferring ownership—you're just letting them read it

A reasonable release form protects them from frivolous lawsuits over general similarities. An unreasonable one asks you to give up your legal rights entirely.

When in doubt, have an entertainment attorney review it. If you can't afford an attorney and the release seems overly broad, you might need to walk away from that opportunity.

CHAPTER 23

THE WGA: GETTING IN AND WHAT IT MEANS

THE WRITERS GUILD of America carries enormous weight in the screenwriting world. It's the union for professional screenwriters, and membership is both a badge of legitimacy and a practical necessity for anyone serious about a screenwriting career.

But here's the catch: You can't just join. You can't work your way in. You can't apply like it's a professional association. You have to earn membership through work—specifically, through work for WGA signatory companies.

And until you do, you're working without a safety net.

WHAT IS THE WGA?

The Writers Guild of America is actually two separate but related unions: WGA West, covering writers west of the Mississippi, and WGA East, covering writers east of the Mississippi. For practical purposes, most film and TV writers deal with WGA West, headquartered in Los Angeles.

The Guild is a labor union that represents writers in negotiations with studios, networks and production companies. It establishes minimum payments, working conditions, credit determination and residuals for its members.

Think of it as the difference between working construction with OSHA protections, workers' comp and union wages, versus working construction under the table for whatever rate someone feels like paying you.

HOW YOU ACTUALLY JOIN THE WGA

Entry is based on a points system. You need to accumulate 24 "units" of credit within three years. Different types of writing earn different unit values:

- Selling or optioning an original screenplay to a signatory company: 24 units (instant qualification)
- Writing a theatrical screenplay on assignment: 24 units (instant qualification)
- Writing a story for a theatrical motion picture: 12 units
- Writing a teleplay for long-form TV (90-plus minutes): 24 units
- Writing a teleplay for a TV pilot (30 to 60 minutes): two units
- Writing a story or teleplay for an episode of TV: one to four units (depending on length and whether you wrote the story, teleplay, or both)
- Rewrite or polish work: Various units depending on the project type

SIGNATORY COMPANIES

The crucial detail: Your work only counts if it's for a company that's signed the WGA's Minimum Basic Agreement (MBA).

This includes all major studios, most production companies and streaming platforms like Netflix, Amazon and Apple TV+.

If you write a screenplay for an independent producer who isn't a WGA signatory, it doesn't count toward membership. If you sell a script to Netflix, it counts immediately.

Once you have 24 units, you become eligible to join. You'll pay an initiation fee (currently $2,500 for WGA West, though it can be paid in installments) plus the first membership dues payment (currently 1.5 percent of your writing income, with minimum and maximum amounts).

Automatic membership: In some cases, if a signatory company wants to hire you for a writing assignment, they can make you WGA-eligible immediately through what's called a "qualification employment." This allows them to bring you into the Guild so they can legally hire you under WGA rules.

THE BENEFITS OF WGA MEMBERSHIP

Once you're in the Guild, you get significant protections and benefits:

Minimum Payments

The WGA establishes minimum compensation for all types of writing work. Minimums for theatrical screenplays start around $100,000-plus for high-budget films (budgets over $5 million). For low-budget films, minimums are lower but still substantial. These amounts change slightly every three years.

For television, minimums vary by episode length, type of program and whether it's network, cable or streaming. A half-hour network comedy episode might have a minimum around $30,000 to $40,000.

These are minimums. Established writers earn far more.

But at least you know you won't be exploited with a $5,000 offer for a feature screenplay from a major studio.

Residuals

Residuals are ongoing payments when your work is reused. If a movie you wrote plays on cable TV, you get paid. If a TV episode you wrote gets streamed, you get paid. These can add up to substantial income over time, especially for successful shows that go into syndication or become streaming staples.

Residuals are one of the most valuable benefits of WGA membership and something non-Guild writers almost never receive.

Health Insurance and Pension

The Guild provides health insurance for members who meet minimum earnings thresholds. Given that healthcare in the United States is catastrophically expensive, this is a huge benefit for freelance writers who wouldn't otherwise have employer-provided insurance.

There's also a pension plan that your employers pay into based on your earnings. This creates retirement security in a profession that doesn't have traditional employment structure.

Credit

If there's a dispute about who should receive writing credit on a film, the WGA conducts credit arbitration. A panel of Guild members reads all drafts and determines who gets credit based on their contributions.

This prevents producers from giving their cousins a credit

for fixing some typos or an actor from demanding a writing credit for a few improvised lines.

Credit matters enormously—it affects your residuals, your reputation and your career trajectory. Having an objective arbitration process protects writers from being screwed out of the credit they deserve.

Legal Support

The Guild provides legal assistance for contract disputes, credit issues and payment problems. If a producer refuses to pay you, the Guild can intervene on your behalf.

The Guild also lobbies for writers' interests in Washington, negotiates industry-wide agreements with studios and fights for better working conditions across the industry.

Community

Guild membership connects you with other professional writers. There are screenings, panels, workshops and networking events. You're part of a community of people doing the same work at the same level.

This might sound touchy-feely, but in a profession where you spend most of your time alone in a room making up stories, having a professional community matters.

The Catch-22

Here's the frustrating paradox: You can't join the Guild until you've worked on Guild-signatory projects, but many Guild-signatory companies prefer to hire Guild writers.

This means you often have to work on non-Guild projects first—building your credits, your reel and your reputation—

until you're good enough that a signatory company wants to hire you. Then you can qualify for membership.

During this period, you're working without protections, often for little or no money, hoping to eventually level up to Guild-protected work.

HOW TO BRIDGE THE GAP

So how do you survive and build a career before you're WGA?

Independent films: Write and sell scripts to independent producers. The pay is low (or nonexistent) but you're building credits and samples. Just make sure you have solid contracts protecting your rights.

Contests and fellowships: Enter major contests and fellowship programs that are taken seriously by people in the industry, such as the Nicholl Fellowship and the Austin Film Festival. Winners and finalists often get meetings with agents, managers and producers.

Shorts and web content: Produce your own short films or web series. This proves you can execute and gives you something to show potential representatives.

Networking up: Every industry relationship you build gets you one step closer to someone who can hire you for Guild-qualified work. Attend industry events, take meetings and be professional and personable.

Day job: Keep a flexible day job that pays your bills while you build your screenwriting career. Most non-Guild writers are not making a living from screenwriting alone.

Protect yourself: Even without Guild protection, get everything in writing. Use solid contracts. Register your work. Don't give away rights if you don't have to.

If you're eligible to join the WGA, should you do it immediately?

Reasons to join right away:

- You have ongoing work with signatory companies.
- You're being offered WGA-covered assignments.
- You need the health insurance.
- You want the credit protection and residuals.

Reasons to wait:

- You're still doing a lot of non-Guild work that you'd have to stop.
- You can't afford the initiation fee.
- You're not sure you'll earn enough to justify the dues.

Most writers join as soon as they're eligible, but it's a personal calculation based on your specific situation.

INTERNATIONAL

If you're outside the United States, the WGA may not be

directly relevant to you. Many countries have their own screen-writer guilds or unions:

- Writers' Guild of Great Britain (WGGB)
- Writers Guild of Canada (WGC)
- Australian Writers' Guild (AWG)

These organizations provide similar protections within their jurisdictions, but if you're writing for American productions you may need to interact with the WGA even if you're based elsewhere.

THE BOTTOM LINE

The Writers Guild of America is the professional standard for screenwriters. Membership provides crucial protections, minimum payments, residuals, healthcare and credit arbitration.

Your goal as an emerging screenwriter should be to build toward Guild eligibility. Write great scripts. Enter respected contests. Network strategically. Take any legitimate opportunities to work with Guild signatory companies.

The difference between being a WGA writer and a non-WGA writer isn't just about money—though the money matters. It's about being a professional with protections versus being an amateur hoping someone doesn't screw you over.

CHAPTER 24

TV PITCH TEMPLATE

AFTER SELLING a show to Lionsgate TV, I was taught by their excellent executives how to pitch a show to streamers and networks. The process is simple: You go in and literally pitch your show.

This is the format. The goal is to cover the core information in eight to 10 minutes.

You want to give a quick, concise pitch, then use the rest of the hour to discuss the show conversationally with the buyer or executives. This makes them part of the process, instead of talking at them for an hour with a pitch that's too long and exhausting.

Visual elements are always encouraged.

Here's the format to follow:

Concept
This is your elevator pitch. Keep it short, conversational and big picture. Don't get lost in the weeds.

Main Characters

Go into detail. Cover backstory, who your main characters are, what makes them tick and what their goals are. Do a deep dive here—TV is all about the characters viewers follow from week to week.

Only cover one to three characters: your leads. You can also include how these characters' relationships grow or fall apart during the early part of the show.

Secondary Characters

List your main secondary characters. Dedicate just one paragraph to each. Include a sentence or two about their relationships to the leads. Only list three or four at most. Remember: Your audience is the buyers. Don't bury them in description—get to the point and show how these characters expand the world of the show.

Why Now

Explain why the story begins at this particular moment. For example: In *Designated Survivor*, the president and his entire cabinet are killed in the pilot, forcing the HUD Secretary (Kiefer Sutherland) to suddenly become president. That's a clear and compelling reason to start telling the story.

The World

Describe the world your show inhabits. If it's a mob show, explain the criminal underworld. If it's sci-fi, explain the rules of the universe. If it's everyday America, describe the environment your characters live in. Show how this world creates tension for the characters and their relationships.

The Pilot

Walk through the pilot, starting with the opening. Then cover five or six major plot points. Don't overload with detail—you want buyers to know you've thought through the pilot, but not overwhelm them.

Make sure the pilot ends on a strong beat filled with tension and unresolved issues, setting up the future of the series.

Early in Season One

Break the season into three sections. After the pilot, set up the early conflicts of the series. Provide four or five beats in moderate detail.

Mid-Season One

Go into slightly less detail than the early section. Outline four or five more events. Show how relationships change and conflicts deepen. Focus more on the characters' journeys than just plot points.

End of Season One

Cover two or three major events, including the finale. Show how the ending sets up conflict for Season Two. Keep it brief— buyers mainly want to see that your season ends with a hook strong enough to bring audiences back.

Season Two

Cover five or six beats quickly—maybe two sentences each. This should be fast. Also, weave in a brief note about where the show is heading overall and how it might end. Buyers just want to know you've thought through the long-term arc. (Truth is, if you're lucky enough to sell the show, your ending will change a hundred times anyway.)

Closing Notes

Finish quickly and leave plenty of time for conversation. Let the buyers ask questions and answer them with confidence. Be precise but not overwhelming.

CHAPTER 25

A FINAL NOTE

No one owes you a career in screenwriting.

THE BUSINESS DOESN'T CARE how talented you are, how long you struggled or how badly you want it. It rewards usefulness, reliability and timing—often in that order. You'll be told no more than yes. You'll be rewritten, replaced, ignored, underpaid and sometimes credited only in spirit. You'll spend years learning how to write scripts and even longer learning how to survive the machinery wrapped around them. If you're still here after all that, it's because something in you refuses to quit.

And yet—if you can do this for a living—it's the best job in the world. You get paid to invent characters, worlds and problems that didn't exist yesterday. You get to collaborate with wildly talented, deeply flawed humans and watch something that once lived only in your head flicker to life on a screen. It's unstable, unfair and occasionally brutal—but it definitely beats having a "real" job.

So choose it with open eyes. And if you manage to make a living telling stories, don't forget how rare that is.

ACKNOWLEDGMENTS

Thank you to Dario Argento, Abel Ferrara, John Carpenter, and all the other filmmakers I've worked with along the way— for treating me as a peer and consistently supporting my work as a screenwriter. Thanks as well to Chris Gore, *Film Threat*, *Film Courage*, and everyone who's invited me onto their platforms and trusted me to speak honestly about Hollywood and the film business.

Special thanks to my girlfriend, Anna David, and the entire Legacy Launch Pad team—Serena Samaha, Arran Skinner, and Mac Durston—for helping bring this book into the world. And finally, thank you to the little bud, Bennie, for reminding me every day that getting a film made isn't the most important thing in life.

ABOUT THE AUTHOR

Jim Agnew is a screenwriter and producer whose work spans action, thriller, noir and other genre-driven storytelling. Known for developing commercially driven genre films that travel well internationally, Agnew is skilled at working within tight budgets and challenging production environments.

In addition to his produced credits, Agnew continues to develop original film and television projects while remaining actively involved in the business side of filmmaking, including financing, production strategy and international co-productions. *To Live and Write in LA* is his first book.

FOR MORE INFORMATION